Also by Scott Russell Sanders

HUNTING FOR HOPE

A FATHER'S JOURNEYS

Scott Russell Sanders

BEACON PRESS

BOSTON

BEACON PRESS
25 Beacon Street, Boston, Massachusetts 02108-2892
www.beacon.org

BEACON PRESS BOOKS
are published under the auspices of
the Unitarian Universalist Association of Congregations.

03 02   8

This book is printed on acid-free paper that meets the uncoated paper
ANSI/NISO specifications for permanence as revised in 1992.

Text design by Anne Chalmers
Composition by Wilsted & Taylor Publishing Services

Library of Congress Cataloging-in-Publication Data

Sanders, Scott R. (Scott Russell), 1945–
Hunting for hope : a father's journeys / Scott Russell Sanders.
      p.   cm.
ISBN 0-8070-6324-X (cloth)
ISBN 0-8070-6425-4 (paper)
I. Title.
PS3569.A5137H86   1998
813'.54—dc21

FOR EVA AND JESSE

If they will listen, sing them a song.
If not, keep silent.
Don't try to break down their door.
        —Confucius

The beauty of the world gives
us an intimation of its claim to
a place in our heart.
        —Simone Weil

I have undertaken, not to see differently from
others, but to look further than others, and
whilst they are busied for the morrow only, I
have turned my thoughts to the whole future.
        —Alexis de Tocqueville

Contents

ONE

WHERE THE
SEARCH BEGINS

SUPPOSE YOUR DAUGHTER is engaged to be married and she asks whether you think she ought to have children, given the sorry state of the world. Suppose your son is starting college and he asks what you think he should study, or why he should study at all, when the future looks so bleak. Or suppose you are a teacher and one student after another comes to ask you how to deal with despair. What would you tell them?

My children and my students have put those questions to me—haltingly, earnestly—and I feel that I owe them an answer. They are not asking for assurances of pie in the sky, for magic pills or guardian angels, for stories ending happily ever after, but for real and present reasons to face the future with confidence.

Let me make it clear that these young people are not depressed, although each of them could name friends who are, for an epidemic of depression is sweeping through their generation. I have met that illness and many who suffer from it; I know its contours and dark recesses. I am speaking here of something else. My son and daughter and, so far as I can tell, the students who pose these questions are bright, healthy, stable, and competent. They have every reason for confidence in themselves; it is the earth they brood about, the outlook for life.

They worry about more than their own private futures, their

prospects for jobs and marriage and happiness; they worry about the future of our whole motley species, our fellow creatures, and the planet. I will not belabor the causes for their concern, will not try to demonstrate the menace posed by nuclear weapons, population growth, pollution, extinction, or global warming. I will not cite the dismal numbers about divorce and poverty, about crime and random cruelty. I will not rehearse the dangers of technology run askew from human purpose, the vacuity of mass media devoted to sales pitches and cheap thrills, the sterility of a life given over to the pursuit of money and toys.

Others have offered those warnings, fervently and cogently, in books and magazines and films, and anyone who is paying attention has already heard the bad news. "One of the penalties of an ecological education," Aldo Leopold remarks, "is that one lives alone in a world of wounds." The young people who put their disturbing questions to me have had an ecological education, and a political one as well. They know we are in trouble. Everywhere they look they see ruined landscapes and ravaged communities and broken people. So they are asking me if I believe we have the resources for healing the wounds, for mending the breaks. They are asking me if I live in hope.

The question has forced me to search the depths of my own fears and beliefs. Coming up with an answer that I can stand by and pass on to those I love is the hardest job I have ever attempted. I can offer no grand theory, no philosophy or theology, no checklist of ten quick ways to save the earth. I deal instead in memories, images, hunches, and tales, all drawn from the muddle of ordinary life.

When the Shawnee and Chippewa and other early people of my region went on hunts or vision quests or long journeys, each traveler would carry in a small rawhide pouch various tokens of spiritual power—a feather, a bit of fur, a claw, a carved root, a pinch of tobacco, a pebble, a shell. These were not simply magical charms; they were reminders of the energies that sustain all life. By gathering these talismans into a medicine pouch, the hunter, traveler, or visionary seeker was recollecting the sources of healing and bounty and beauty. I have gathered here my own medicine bundle, tokens made of words instead of bark or bone, to honor the powers in nature, in culture, in community, in my depths and in yours, that nourish and heal.

Not easily, not without battling despair, I *do* live in hope. This book is my effort to say as clearly as I can where that hope is grounded. I have struggled for several years over the writing. During all that labor, the book seemed to be nearby yet inaccessible, like a bundle I could not untie, like a locked house whose floor plan and furnishings I knew but for which I had no key. Then one morning I came bright awake at 3:00 A.M., hearing the sentence "Let me tell you a story." Immediately I felt certain that here was the key to open my locked book. First I heard the words inwardly, then I whispered them into the darkness. Only my wife's steady breathing from the next pillow kept me from shouting: "Let me tell you a story!"

Even in the sober light of dawn, which usually bleaches the glamour from my dreamtime revelations, and even when I wrote down the sentence and stared at it hard, I still felt as though I had found the key. So I begin with a story, as a way of setting out in search of hope.

TWO

MOUNTAIN
MUSIC I

ON A JUNE MORNING high in the Rocky Mountains of Colorado, snowy peaks rose before me like the promise of a world without grief. A creek brim full of meltwater roiled along to my left, and to my right an aspen grove shimmered with new leaves. Bluebirds darted in and out of holes in the aspen trunks, and butterflies flickered beside every puddle, tasting the succulent mud. Sun glazed the new grass and licked a silver sheen along the boughs of pines.

With all of that to look at, I gazed instead at my son's broad back as he stalked away from me up the trail. Sweat had darkened his gray T-shirt in patches the color of bruises. His shoulders were stiff with anger that would weight his tongue and keep his face turned from me for hours. Anger also made him quicken his stride, gear after gear, until I could no longer keep up. I had forty-nine years on my legs and heart and lungs, while Jesse had only seventeen on his. My left foot ached from old bone breaks and my right knee creaked from recent surgery. Used to breathing among the low, muggy hills of Indiana, I was gasping up here in the alpine air, a mile and a half above sea level. Jesse would not stop, would not even slow down unless I asked; and I was in no mood to ask. So I slumped against a boulder beside the trail and let him rush on ahead.

. . .

This day, our first full one in Rocky Mountain National Park, had started out well. I woke at first light, soothed by the roar of a river foaming along one edge of the campground, and looked out from our tent to find half a dozen elk, all cows and calves, grazing so close by that I could see the gleam of their teeth. Just beyond the elk, a pair of ground squirrels loafed at the lip of their burrow, noses twitching. Beyond the squirrels, a ponderosa pine, backlit by sunrise, caught the wind in its ragged limbs. The sky was a blue slate marked only by the curving flight of swallows.

Up to that point, and for several hours more, the day was equally unblemished. Jesse slept on while I sipped coffee and studied maps and soaked in the early light. We made our plans over breakfast without squabbling: walk to Bridal Veil Falls in the morning, raft on the Cache la Poudre River in the afternoon, return to camp in the evening to get ready for backpacking up into Wild Basin the next day. Tomorrow we would be heavily laden, but today we carried only water and snacks, and I felt buoyant as we hiked along Cow Creek toward the waterfall. We talked easily the whole way, joking and teasing, more like good friends than like father and son. Yet even as we sat at the base of the falls, our shoulders touching, the mist of Bridal Veil cooling our skin, we remained father and son, locked in a struggle that I could only partly understand.

For the previous year or so, no matter how long our spells of serenity, Jesse and I had kept falling into quarrels, like victims of malaria breaking out in fever. We might be talking about soccer or supper, about the car keys or the news, and suddenly our voices would begin to clash like swords. I had proposed this trip to the mountains in hopes of discovering the source of that strife. Of course I knew that teenage sons and their fathers are expected to fight, yet I sensed there was a grievance between us that ran deeper than the usual vexations. Jesse was troubled by more than a desire to run his own life, and I was troubled by more than the pain of letting him go. I wished to track our anger to its lair, to find where it hid and fed and grew, and then, if I could not slay the demon, at least I could drag it into the light and call it by name.

The peace between us held until we turned back from the waterfall and began discussing where to camp the following night. Jesse wanted to push on up to Thunder Lake, near eleven thousand feet, and pitch our tent on snow. I wanted to stop a thousand feet lower and sleep on dry dirt.

"We're not equipped for snow," I told him.

"Sure we are. Why do you think I bought a new sleeping bag? Why did I call ahead to reserve snowshoes?"

I suggested that we could hike up from a lower campsite and snowshoe to his heart's content.

He loosed a snort of disgust. "I can't believe you're wimping out on me, Dad."

"I'm just being sensible."

"You're wimping out. I came here to see the backcountry, and all you want to do is poke around the foothills."

"This isn't wild enough for you?" I waved my arms at the view. "What do you need—avalanches and grizzlies?"

Just then, as we rounded a bend, an elderly couple came shuffling toward us, hunched over walking sticks, white hair jutting from beneath their straw hats. They were followed by three toddling children, each rigged out with tiny backpack and canteen. Jesse and I stood aside to let them pass, returning nods to their cheery hellos.

After they had trooped by, Jesse muttered, "We're in the wilds, huh, Dad? That's why the trail's full of grandparents and kids." Then he quickened his pace until the damp blond curls that dangled below his billed cap were slapping against his neck.

"Is this how it's going to be?" I called after him. "You're going to spoil the trip because I won't agree to camp on snow?"

He turned and glared at me. "You're the one who's spoiling it, you and your hang-ups. You always ruin everything."

With that, he swung his face away and lengthened his stride

and rushed on ahead. I watched his rigid shoulders and the bruise-colored patches on the back of his T-shirt until he disappeared beyond a rise. That was when I gave up on chasing him, slumped against a boulder, and sucked at the thin air. Butterflies dallied around my boots and hawks kited on the breeze, but they might have been blips on a screen, and the whole panorama of snowy peaks and shimmering aspens and shining pines might have been cut from cardboard, for all the feeling they stirred in me.

The rocks that give these mountains their name are ancient, nearly a third as old as the earth, but the Rockies themselves are new, having been lifted up only six or seven million years ago, and they were utterly new to me, for I had never seen them before except from airplanes. I had been yearning toward them since I was Jesse's age, had been learning about their natural and human history, the surge of stone and gouge of glaciers, the wandering of hunters and wolves. Drawn to these mountains from the rumpled quilt of fields and forests in the hill country of the Ohio Valley, I was primed for splendor. And yet now that I was here I felt blinkered and numb.

What we call landscape is a stretch of earth overlaid with memory, expectation, and thought. Land is everything that is actually *there*, independent of us; landscape is what we allow in through the doors of perception. My own doors had slammed shut. My quarrel with Jesse changed nothing about the Rockies, but changed everything in my experience of the place. What had seemed glorious and vibrant when we set out that morning now seemed bleak and bare. It was as though anger had drilled a hole in the world and leached the color away.

I was still simmering when I caught up with Jesse at the trail head, where he was leaning against our rented car, arms crossed over his chest, head sunk forward in a sullen pose I knew all too well, eyes hidden beneath the frayed bill of his cap. Having to wait for me to unlock the car had no doubt reminded him of another gripe: I carried the only set of keys. Because he was too young to be covered by the rental company's insurance, I would not let him drive. He had fumed about my decision, interpreting it as proof that I mistrusted him, still thought of him as a child. That earlier scuffle had petered out with him grumbling, "Stupid, stupid. I knew this would happen. Why did I come out here? Why?"

The arguments all ran together, playing over and over in my head as we jounced, too fast, along a rutted gravel road toward the highway. The tires whumped and the small engine whined up hills and down, but the silence inside the car was louder. We had two hours of driving to our rendezvous spot for the rafting trip, and I knew that Jesse could easily clamp his jaw shut for that long, and longer. I glanced over at him from time to time, looking for any sign of detente. His eyes were glass.

We drove. In the depths of Big Thompson Canyon, where the road swerved along a frothy river between sheer rockface and spindly guardrail, I could bear the silence no longer. "So what are my hang-ups?" I demanded. "How do I ruin everything?"

"You don't want to know," he said.

"I want to know. What is it about me that grates on you?"

I do not pretend to recall the exact words we hurled at one another after my challenge, but I remember the tone and thrust of them, and here is how they have stayed with me:

"You wouldn't understand," he said.

"Try me."

He cut a look at me, shrugged, then stared back through the windshield. "You're just so out of touch."

"With what?"

"With my whole world. You hate everything that's fun. You hate television and movies and video games. You hate my music."

"I like some of your music. I just don't like it loud."

"You hate advertising," he said quickly, rolling now. "You hate billboards and lotteries and developers and logging companies and big corporations. You hate snowmobiles and jet skis. You hate malls and fashions and cars."

"You're still on my case because I won't buy a Jeep?" I said, harking back to another old argument.

"Forget Jeeps. You look at any car and all you think is pollution, traffic, roadside crap. You say fast-food's poisoning our bodies and TV's poisoning our minds. You think the Internet is just another scam for selling stuff. You think business is a conspiracy to rape the earth."

"None of that bothers you?"

"Of course it does. But that's the *world*. That's where we've got to live. It's not going to go away just because you don't approve. What's the good of spitting on it?"

"I don't spit on it. I grieve over it."

He was still for a moment, then resumed quietly. "What's the good of grieving if you can't change anything?"

"Who says you can't change anything?"

"*You* do. Maybe not with your mouth, but with your eyes." Jesse rubbed his own eyes, and the words came out muffled through his cupped palms. "Your view of things is totally dark. It bums me out. You make me feel the planet's dying and people are to blame and nothing can be done about it. There's no room for hope. Maybe you can get by without hope, but I can't. I've got a lot of living still to do. I have to believe there's a way we can get out of this mess. Otherwise what's the point? Why study, why work—why do anything if it's all going to hell?"

That sounded unfair to me, a caricature of my views, and I thought of many sharp replies; yet there was too much truth and too much hurt in what he said for me to fire back an answer. Had I really deprived my son of hope? Was this the deeper grievance—that I had passed on to him, so young, my anguish over the world? Was this what lurked between us, driving us apart, the demon called despair?

"You're right," I finally told him. "Life's meaningless without hope. But I think you're wrong to say I've given up."

"It seems that way to me. As if you think we're doomed."

"No, buddy, I don't think we're doomed. It's just that nearly everything I care about is under assault."

"See, that's what I mean. You're so worried about the fate of the earth, you can't enjoy anything. We come to these mountains and you bring the shadows with you. You've got me seeing nothing but darkness."

Stunned by the force of his words, I could not speak. If my gloom cast a shadow over Creation for my son, then I had failed him. What remedy could there be for such a betrayal?

Through all the shouting and then talking and then the painful hush, our car hugged the swerving road, yet I cannot remember steering. I cannot remember seeing the stony canyon, the white mane of the Big Thompson whipping along beside us, the oncoming traffic. Somehow we survived our sashay with the river and cruised into a zone of burger joints and car-care emporiums and trinket shops. I realized how often, how relentlessly, I had groused about just this sort of "commercial dreck," and how futile my complaints must have seemed to Jesse.

He was caught between a chorus of voices telling him that the universe was made for us—that the earth is an inexhaustible warehouse, that consumption is the goal of life, that money is the road to delight—and the stubborn voice of his father saying none of this is so. If his father was right, then much of what humans babble every day—in ads and editorials, in sitcoms and song lyrics, in thrillers and market reports and teenage gab—is a monstrous lie. Far more likely that his father was wrong, deluded, perhaps even mad.

We observed an unofficial truce for the rest of the way to the gas station north of Fort Collins, where we met the rafting crew at noon. There had been record rains and snowfall in the Rockies for the previous three months, so every brook and river tumbling down from the mountains was frenzied and fast. When local people heard that we meant to raft the Cache la Poudre in this rough season they frowned and advised against it, recounting stories of broken legs, crushed skulls, deaths. Seeing that we were determined to go, they urged us to settle for the shorter trip that joined the river below the canyon, where the water spread out and calmed down. But Jesse had his heart set on taking the wildest ride available, so we had signed up for the twelve-mile trip through the boulder-strewn canyon.

I was relieved to see that the crowd of twenty or so waiting at the rendezvous point included scrawny kids and rotund parents. If the outfitters were willing to haul such passengers, how risky could the journey be? The sky-blue rafts, stacked on trailers behind yellow vans, looked indestructible. The guides seemed edgy, however, as they told us what to do if we were flung into the river, how to survive a tumble over rocks, how to get out from under a flipped raft, how to drag a flailing comrade back on board.

Jesse stood off by himself and listened to these dire instructions with a sober face. I could see him preparing, gaze focused inward, lips tight, the way he concentrated before taking his place in goal at a soccer game.

When the time came for us to board the vans, he and I turned out to be the only customers for the canyon run; all the others, the reedy kids and puffing parents, were going on the tamer trip. Our raft would be filled out by three sinewy young men, students at Colorado State who were being paid to risk their necks: a guide with a year's experience and two trainees.

The water in Poudre Canyon looked murderous, all spume and standing waves and suckholes and rips. Every cascade, every low bridge, every jumble of boulders reminded the guides of some disaster which they rehearsed with gusto. It was part of their job to crank up the thrill, I knew that, but I also knew from talking with friends that most of the tales were true.

At the launching spot, Jesse and I wriggled into our black wet-suits, cinched tight the orange flotation vests, buckled on white helmets. The sight of my son in that armor sent a blade of anxiety through me again. What if he got hurt? Lord God, what if he were killed?

"Hey, Dad," Jesse called, hoisting a paddle in his fist, "you remember how to use one of these?"

"Seems like I remember teaching *you*," I called back.

He flashed me a grin, the first sign of communion since we had sat with shoulders touching in the mist of Bridal Veil Falls. That one look restored me to my senses, and I felt suddenly the dazzle of sunlight, heard the river's rumble and the fluting of birds, smelled pine sap and wet stone.

One of the trainees, a lithe wisecracker named Harry, would guide our run. "If it gets quiet in back," he announced, "that means I've fallen in and somebody else better take over."

We clambered into the raft—Jesse and I up front, the veteran guide and the other trainee in the middle, Harry in the stern. Each of us hooked one foot under a loop sewn into the rubbery floor, jammed the other foot under a thwart. Before we hit the first rapids, Harry made us practice synchronizing our strokes as he hollered, "Back paddle! Forward paddle! Stop! Left turn! Right turn!" The only other command, he explained, was "Jump!" Hearing that, the paddlers on the side away from some looming boulder or snag were to heave themselves *toward* the obstruction, in order to keep the raft from flipping.

"I know it sounds crazy," said Harry. "But it works. And remember: from now on, if you hear fear in my voice, it's real."

Fear was all I felt over the next few minutes, a bit for myself and a lot for Jesse, as we struck white water and the raft began to buck. Waves slammed against the bow, spray flew, stone whizzed by. A bridge swelled ahead of us, water boiling under the low arches, and Harry shouted, "Duck!" then steered us between the lethal pilings and out the other side into more rapids, where he yelled, "Left turn! Dig hard! Harder!"

He kept barking orders, and soon I was too busy paddling to feel anything except my own muscles pulling against the great writhing muscle of the river. I breathed in as much water as air. The raft spun and dipped and leapt with ungainly grace, sliding through narrow flumes, gliding over rocks, kissing cliffs and bouncing away, yielding to the grip of the current and springing free. Gradually I sank into my body.

The land blurred past. Sandstone bluffs rose steeply along one shore, then the other, then both—hundreds of feet of rock pinching the sky high above into a ribbon of blue. Here and there a terrace opened, revealing a scatter of junipers and scrub cedars, yet before I could spy what else might be growing there it jerked away out of sight. I could tell only that this was dry country, harsh and spare, with dirt the color of scrap iron and gouged by erosion. Every time I tried to fix on a detail, on bird or flower or stone, a shout from Harry yanked me back to the swing of the paddle.

The point of our bucking ride, I realized, was not to *see* the canyon but to survive it. The river was our bronco, our bull, and the land through which it flowed was no more present to us than the rodeo's dusty arena to a whirling cowboy. Haste hid the country, dissolved the landscape, as surely as anger or despair ever did.

"Forward paddle!" Harry shouted. "Give me all you've got! We're coming to the Widow-Maker! Let's hope we come out alive!"

The flooded Poudre, surging through its crooked canyon, was a string of emergencies, each one christened with an ominous name. In a lull between rapids I glanced over at Jesse, and he was beaming. His helmet seemed to strain from the expansive pressure of his smile. I laughed aloud to see him. When he was little I could summon that look of unmixed delight into his face merely by coming home, opening my arms, and calling, "Where's my boy?" In his teenage years, the look had become rare, and it hardly ever had anything to do with me.

"Jump!" Harry shouted.

Before I could react, Jesse lunged at me and landed heavily, and the raft bulged over a boulder, nearly tipping, then righted itself and plunged on downstream.

"Good job!" Harry crowed. "That was a close one."

Jesse scrambled back to his post. "You okay?" he asked.

"Sure," I answered. "How about you?"

"Great," he said. "Fantastic."

For the remaining two hours of our romp down the Poudre I kept stealing glances at Jesse, who paddled as though his life truly depended on how hard he pulled. His face shone with joy, and my own joy was kindled from seeing it.

This is an old habit of mine, the watching and weighing of my son's experience. Since his birth I have enveloped him in a cloud of thought. How's he doing? I wonder. Is he hungry? Hurting? Tired? Is he grumpy or glad? Like so many other exchanges between parent and child, this concern flows mainly one way; Jesse does not surround *me* with thought. On the contrary, with each passing year he pays less and less attention to me, except when he needs something, and then he bristles at being reminded of his dependence. That's natural, mostly, although teenage scorn for parents also gets a boost from popular culture. My own father had to die before I thought seriously about what he might have needed or wanted or suffered. If Jesse has children of his own one day, no doubt he will brood on them as I have brooded on him for these seventeen years. Meanwhile, his growing up requires him to break free of my concern. I accept that, yet I cannot turn off my fathering mind.

Before leaving for Colorado, I had imagined that he would be able to meet the Rockies with clear eyes, with the freshness of his green age. So long as he was in my company, however, he would see the land through the weather of my moods. And if despair had so darkened my vision that I was casting a shadow over Jesse's world, even here among these magnificent mountains and tumultuous rivers, then I would have to change. I would have to learn to see differently. Since I could not forget the wounds to people and planet, could not unlearn the dismal numbers—the tallies of pollution and population and poverty that foretold catastrophe—I would have to look harder for antidotes, for medicines, for sources of hope.

Tired and throbbing from the river trip, we scarcely spoke during the long drive back to our campground in the national park. This time, though, the silence felt easy, like a fullness rather than a void.

In that tranquility I recalled our morning's hike to Bridal Veil Falls, before the first quarrel of the day. No matter how briskly I walked, Jesse kept pulling ahead. He seemed to be in a race, eyes focused far up the trail, as though testing himself against the rugged terrain. I had come to this high country for a holiday from rushing. A refugee from the tyranny of deadlines and destinations, I wished to linger, squatting over the least flower or fern, reading the braille of bark with my fingers, catching the notes of water and birds and wind. But Jesse was just as intent on covering ground. Although we covered the same ground, most of the time we experienced quite different landscapes, his charged with trials of endurance, mine with trials of perception. Then every once in a while the land brought us together—in the mist of the falls, on the back of the river—and it was as if, for a moment, the same music played in both of us.

Without any quarrel to distract me, I watched the road faithfully as we wound our way up through Big Thompson Canyon. We entered the park at dusk. A rosy light glinted on the frozen peaks of the Front Range.

I was driving slowly, on the lookout for wildlife, when a coyote loped onto the road ahead of us, paused halfway across, then stared back in the direction from which it had come. As we rolled to a stop, a female elk came charging after, head lowered and teeth bared. The coyote bounded away, scooted up a bank on the far side of the road, then paused to peer back over its bony shoulder. Again the elk charged; again the coyote pranced away, halted, stared. Jesse and I watched this ballet of taunting and chasing, taunting and chasing, until the pair vanished over a ridge.

"What was that all about?" he asked when we drove on.

"She was protecting a calf, I expect."

"You mean a coyote can eat an elk?"

"The newborns they can."

When I shut off the engine at the campground and we climbed out of the car, it was as though we had stepped back into the raft, for the sound of rushing water swept over us. The sound lured us downhill to the bank of a stream and we sat there soaking in the watery music until our bellies growled. We made supper while the full moon chased Jupiter and Mars up the arc of the sky. The flame on our stove flounced in a northerly breeze, promising cool weather for tomorrow's hike into Wild Basin.

We left the flap of our tent open so we could lie on our backs and watch the stars burn fiercely in the mountain air. Our heads were so close together that I could hear Jesse's breath, even above the shoosh of the river, and I could tell he was nowhere near sleep.

"I feel like I'm still on the water," he said after a spell, "and the raft's bobbing under me and the waves are crashing all around."

"I feel it too."

"That's one of the things I wanted to be sure and do before things fall apart."

I rolled onto my side and propped my head on an elbow and looked at his moonlit profile. "Things don't *have* to fall apart, buddy."

"Maybe not." He blinked, and the spark in his eyes went out and relit. "I just get scared."

"So do I. But the earth's a tough old bird. And we should be smart enough to figure out how to live here."

"Let's hope." There was the scritch of a zipper and a thrashing of legs, and Jesse sprawled on top of his new sleeping bag, which was too warm for this fifty-degree night. "I guess things could be scarier," he said. "Imagine being an elk, never knowing what's sneaking up on you."

"Or a coyote," I said, "never knowing where you'll find your next meal."

A great horned owl called. Another answered, setting up a duet across our valley. We listened until they quit.

"You know," said Jesse, "I've been thinking. Maybe we don't need to sleep on snow. Maybe we can pitch camp in the morning at North St. Vrain, where there ought to be some bare ground, then we can snowshoe on up to Thunder Lake in the afternoon."

"You wouldn't be disappointed if we did that? Wouldn't feel we'd wimped out?"

"Naw," he said. "That's cool."

"Then that's the plan, man."

The stars burned on. The moon climbed. Just when I thought he was asleep, Jesse murmured, "How's that knee?"

"Holding up so far," I told him, surprised by the question, and only then did I notice the aching in my knee and foot.

"Glad to hear it. I don't want to be lugging you out of the mountains."

When he was still young enough to ride in a backpack I had lugged him to the tops of mountains and through dripping woods and along the slate beds of creeks and past glittering windows on city streets, while he burbled and sang over my shoulder; but I knew better than to remind him of that now in his muscular youth. I lay quietly, following the twin currents of the river and my son's breath. Here were two reasons for rejoicing, two sources of hope. For Jesse's sake, and for mine, I would get up the next morning and hunt for more.

THREE

LEAPING UP IN EXPECTATION

WHAT SORT OF BIRD are we looking for? Here is how Emily Dickinson describes it:

> "Hope" is the thing with feathers—
> That perches in the soul—
> And sings the tunes without the words—
> And never stops—at all—

These lines capture something of how hope feels: flighty and frail but also tough, resolute, singing on stubbornly through fat times and lean. Anyone who bands migratory warblers, or who picks up a bird stunned from crashing into a window, holds this paradox in the palm of the hand: a quivering wisp that can fly thousands of miles, a speck of life that can burn on steadily through storms.

In spite of Dickinson's testimony, however, the bird may quit singing. The psychiatrist Viktor Frankl tells of having observed, in Nazi concentration camps, the moment when a fellow prisoner gave up hope. The man would go quiet, smoke a last cigarette he had been hoarding, refuse to get out of bed, ignore threats or blows, and soon, usually within a day, the prisoner would die. In the same way, patients who suffer from cancer or AIDS or another deadly disease may lose faith in their recovery, and thus quickly fail. You can see that surrender in the eyes of people wrapped in greasy blankets on our streets; you can see it in the eyes of children bruised by hands or hunger or neglect. And even in circumstances much less dire, anyone who outlives childhood must pass through spells when the inward singing stops.

No understanding of hope can be honest unless it reckons with the absence of hope, the dark night of the soul when nothing comforts and nothing reassures. "I am allotted months of emptiness, and nights of misery are apportioned to me," Job laments, "and I am full of tossing till the dawn." Yet dawn brings Job no relief, for his days are "swifter than a weaver's shuttle, and come to their end without hope." Unless we acknowledge the power of despair, sooner or later it will overwhelm us, if only because we cannot escape our own death or the spectacle of pain. "A man who is not afraid of the sea will soon be drowned," an old fisherman told the Irish poet John Synge, "for he will be going out on a day he shouldn't. But we do be afraid of the sea, and we do only be drownded now and again." Knowing the dangers of the sea will not guarantee our safety; but without such knowledge we will almost surely drown. If hope is a bright, indomitable bird, despair is the dark ocean over which it flies, against which it sings. Likewise, that darkness, that dangerous sea, is the background against which I write.

I used to have a short dog that loved to run in tall grass. Like Dickinson's bird, this mutt sticks with me as an image of hope. He was a mix of breeds, more cocker spaniel than anything else, with floppy ears and lolling tongue and woebegone eyes. My family called him Doby because we could not quite bring ourselves to call him Dopey, which was nearer the truth. We considered him dopey because of his fondness for sleeping on our country road, where the blacktop held the day's warmth long into evening, and because he would eat anything, including shoes and laundry and gloves. Three times he was run over while snoozing stretched out across the humped spine of that road, and three times he survived.

The only thing Doby would rather do than sleep or eat was go for walks. Whenever I stepped outside he would rush to join me, day or night, on a full stomach or an empty one, and he would not stop until I did. When I struck out across a lush hayfield in summer, and the seedheads of the timothy brushed against my waist, Doby would burrow in after me, the grass looming twice his height. Mostly he nosed along at my heels. Then every little while he would race ahead, tongue flailing and ears kiting, gathering speed, and then he would jump, lifting his head for an instant over the tops of the grass. In that instant he was a tall dog, tall enough to see where he was going.

I thought of Doby and his exuberant jump when I discovered that the words *hope* and *hop* come from the same root, one that means "to leap up in expectation." Isn't that how it feels to be hopeful—that buoyancy, that eagerness for what is to come? Since before our ancestors began planting crops, humans have been living in expectation, counting on the hunt and the harvest, on what the earth and our labors will bring forth. We invented ways of speaking about what we plan for or long for, even when it is not yet visible: spring will come, we say, the drought will end, the fever will break; I shall marry you in the moon when the geese fly north, and our children will prosper. All covenants, all vows, all prophecies are cast in the future tense.

When we leap up, what do we see? If we see nothing but shadows closing in, if we expect only disaster, we may well quit leaping altogether. We may hunker down in the present, sink into momentary sensation—not as a way of experiencing the fullness of being, as mystics would have us do, but as a way of avoiding tomorrow. "The prisoner who had lost faith in the future—his future—was doomed," Frankl reports from his time in the Nazi camps. "With his loss of belief in the future, he also lost his spiritual hold; he let himself decline and became subject to mental and physical decay." In a milder but still hazardous form, this is what my children, my students, and many others of their generation are facing.

The first condition of hope is to believe that you will *have* a future; the second is to believe that there will be a decent world in which to live it. What happens when large numbers of young people despair of the future may be judged from the rising rates of drug addiction, alcoholism, promiscuity, suicide, and violent crime among adolescents and teenagers. A Miami detective, asked on radio how he would account for the increasing number of murders committed by children, tells a reporter, "You look in the eyes of these kids, and there's nobody home. There's not a flicker of light." When I held my newborn daughter, and later, my newborn son, I saw the eagerness for life burning in them. If that light—that fire—burns in every healthy infant, as surely it does, then how has it been extinguished in so many children, and how can it be rekindled?

I remember talking with a woman from Chicago who told me she was astonished to have reached the age of thirty. She started doing drugs at ten, joined a gang at twelve, killed a rival and went off to prison at fifteen, and never expected to reach eighteen. What preserved her, she said, was a rehabilitation program that took her and other young inmates on day-trips into the Indiana dunes and on week-long canoe trips into the Boundary Waters of Minnesota. In those wild places she felt safe for the first time in her life: "There was nothing and nobody hating me or wanting to hurt me. Even with all that dirt and sand and rock, those places were clean, they were alive, they looked like they might last." Having seen parts of the earth that promised to endure, she came to believe that she herself might endure, and that belief saved her. Now, at the improbable age of thirty, this woman was leading groups of juvenile offenders on wilderness journeys.

.   .   .

Hearing what I was up to in this book, a friend wrote me a post-card to say, "Hope is like memory in its action: memory grips the past and hope grips the future." Yes, I thought, hope and memory are kindred powers, binding together the scraps of time. We compose the stories of our lives by casting thought backward and forward, remembering and anticipating.

A British couple in their mid-twenties, haggard and bruised, recall for the television camera how they were on holiday in Indonesia, trying to decide whether to get married, when the ferryboat they were riding between islands sank during a storm. They clambered into a lifeboat, but so did many others, and the lifeboat foundered. So the couple set off swimming, calling back and forth to keep track of one another in the rough seas, until they came upon a floating spar, and there they clung, waiting for rescue. Eventually five other passengers joined them; but one by one the others ran out of strength, let go of the spar, and drowned. Asked how they managed to hold on for thirteen hours while the waves hurled them about, the British couple smile shyly at the camera. The woman says, We remembered things we'd done together, we told jokes, we sang. We promised one another we'd get married straightaway, the man says, if only we survived. It seemed almost like a test, the woman says, as though some great power had asked us a question. How could we let go?

My daughter Eva, whom I held as a newborn in the palm of my hand, is now twenty-three and talks of holding her own newborn one day. Like Jesse, now a freshman in college, Eva is radiant with beginnings. She has just begun planning her wedding, just begun studying for a Ph.D. in biology, just moved into her first house. Eagerness for life still burns in Jesse and Eva, and what keeps it alight, now that they are old enough to recognize the larger troubles of the world, is the promise of leading useful, joyful, purposeful lives.

Memory grips the past; hope grips the future. It has become fashionable in some intellectual circles to scorn the idea that one's life might have a coherent plot, with beginning and middle and end, let alone that the universe as a whole might be playing out such a meaningful story. Those who offer the scorn, I notice, often plan their days and careers prudently, watching their diets and compiling resumes and signing contracts and investing in pensions, for all the world as if they believed their lives might add up to something.

No one who has followed the disintegration of an Alzheimer's patient would be likely to mock our struggle for coherence and meaning. Several people close to me have suffered from that disease, and I have watched them lose their grip on the past, as memory dwindles, and on the future, as imagination wanes. Adrift in time, they succumb to disorientation and panic, and, in the final stages, to terror. "Who is that man?" a woman asks about her husband of fifty years. "Who are these people? What are they doing to me?" she asks about the nurses who care for her around the clock. Rocking in his bed, a man says, "I want Ethyl, I want Ethyl." When he is reminded that Ethyl died a long while ago, he balls up his fists and beats on his head and wails, "Why didn't anybody tell me? Why is everything secret?" And so each day his wife dies all over again and again he is plunged into grief. It is as though these Alzheimer's patients are caught down in the tall grass, the spring gone from their minds, unable to leap up and see where they have come from or where they are going.

Many forms of therapy recognize our need to make peace with the past; we are just as much in need of making peace with the future. As long as we are eaten up with confusion or guilt over what has happened, and with anxiety or cynicism over what is to come, we lose our hold on the present—which, as every spiritual tradition teaches us, is where we actually dwell. I belong to a generation that murmured "Be here now" like a mantra. I know that I am alive only in this moment, in this place. And yet, if I am to live fully in the here and now, I must be able to look both backward and forward with clear vision.

·   ·   ·

Only people who are convinced that there can be no relief from misery in *this* world will fix all their hopes on some other one. So the early Christians dreamed of heaven, where they would join the saints to bask in the radiance of God while their persecutors roasted over Satan's fires. Africans who had been enslaved and hauled to America sang of climbing Jacob's Ladder, crossing the River Jordan in the arms of angels, going home to Glory Land. The native peoples of North America, defeated in battle and driven from their lands, stricken by smallpox and starvation, danced their vision of a spirit world where the whites could not follow and the buffalo would be plentiful and the grass would always be green.

When *all* hope is projected beyond death into an afterlife, it becomes a form of despair. In Christian reckoning, despair is a sin, because it signifies a doubting of God's power to intervene in history, yet the New Testament itself often seems to forsake history. One of the most elaborate biblical descriptions of hope appears in the anonymous Letter to the Hebrews: "Now faith is the assurance of things hoped for, the conviction of things not seen. For by it the men of old received divine approval. By faith we understand that the world was created by the word of God, so that what is seen was made out of things which do not appear." So far so good. But then the letter goes on to describe these "men of old" as "strangers and exiles on the earth" who were "seeking a homeland" elsewhere, "a better country, that is, a heavenly one. Therefore God is not ashamed to be called their God, for he has prepared for them a city." One proof of their faith, in other words, is that they have given up on this tainted, fallen earth.

No one is more responsible for this otherworldly strain in Christianity than the apostle Paul. In his famous hymn to the spiritual gifts, love gets first billing, but hope is close behind: "So faith, hope, love abide, these three; but the greatest of these is love." What sort of hope Paul had in mind may be gathered from reading his letters, as when he tells the Colossians, "We always thank God, the Father of our Lord Jesus Christ, when we pray for you, because we have heard of your faith in Christ Jesus and of the love which you have for all the saints, because of the hope laid up for you in heaven."

Paul's otherworldly sentiments still echo in our own time, often with devastating results. President Reagan's Secretary of the Interior, James Watt, once publicly remarked that there was no need to conserve the forests because God will be coming to judge the quick and the dead long before we can use up all those trees. Battling insomnia one night, I tuned in a televangelist who quoted the Book of Revelations to prove that AIDS and acid rain and ethnic wars are welcome signs of the coming Rapture, when the faithful will be snatched up bodily into heaven. On a lawn outside the building where I teach in southern Indiana, a preacher often shouts at students to beware of reading any book except the Bible, because the only future they need prepare for is the hour when God will divide the saved from the damned.

Such a fixation on the afterlife has provoked many intellectuals to dismiss all religious hope as nothing more than snake oil for the afflicted. Thus Voltaire, in his *Philosophical Dictionary*, defined hope as a "Christian virtue which consists in our despising all poor things here below in expectation of enjoying in an unknown country unknown joys which our priests promise us for the worth of our money." A similar view led Marx to call religion the opiate of the people, a drug that eases the ache of history by focusing our aspirations on eternity. "Hope is the worst of evils," according to Nietzsche, "for it prolongs the torment of man." And H. L. Mencken described hope as "a pathological belief in the occurrence of the impossible."

Granted, peddlers of snake oil do walk among us. But their otherworldly version of hope is not the only one, nor the most compelling, to be found in the Bible. When the prophet Amos cried, "Let justice roll down like waters, and righteousness like an ever-flowing stream," he meant right there in Israel, right then in the reign of King Jeroboam. When Isaiah prophesied that warring peoples "shall beat their swords into plowshares, and their spears into pruning hooks; nation shall not lift up sword against nation, neither shall they learn war any more," he was aiming his words at Israel and her belligerent neighbors.

Salvation and *savior* come from a root which means to heal, to make whole. Whatever Jesus may have promised about spiritual salvation, the New Testament shows him working to heal people in the flesh. Some of the words attributed to him do point beyond flesh and history—"You are from below, I am from above; you are of this world, I am not of this world"—yet his *actions* respond to the needs of his time and place. Again and again he touches the blind, the lame, the humiliated, telling them, Arise and go, your faith has made you whole. He feeds the hungry, reconciles enemies, restores sanity to those who are mad, demands generosity from the rich and mercy from the powerful. "Thy kingdom come," he teaches his followers to pray, "Thy will be done, on earth as it is in heaven." Not content to wait for eternity to bring about the reign of God, Jesus works for justice, peace, and loving community here and now.

An old proverb warns that anyone who feeds on hope will die fasting. And indeed we will starve if our bread is baked from air. If we are to be nourished by hope, it must be grounded in real sources, common sources, ones available not only to heroes and saints, but to everyone, everywhere. To base our lives on a belief in the impossible, as Mencken acidly observed, is to live in delusion. But it would be just as foolish to hold too narrow a view of what is possible.

After Vaclav Havel was released from the last in a series of prison terms for his protests against the Communist regime in Czechoslovakia, and well before the democratic revolution that would overthrow that regime and raise him to the presidency, he told an interviewer, "I think that the deepest and most important form of hope, the only one that can keep us above water and urge us to good works, and the only true source of the breathtaking dimension of the human spirit and its efforts, is something we get, as it were, from 'elsewhere.'" For years, Havel and his fellow dissidents had been circulating petitions, drafting manifestos, staging protest plays, smuggling news to the outside world, with very little to show for it aside from their prison records. What kept them struggling? Not a belief that their cause would prevail, but a belief that their cause was right. "Hope is definitely not the same thing as optimism," Havel explained. "Hope is not prognostication. It is an orientation of the spirit, an orientation of the heart; it transcends the world that is immediately experienced, and is anchored somewhere beyond its horizons." Havel's actions make clear that he was not saying that our hope should be *invested* elsewhere, in heaven or a utopian future, but that it *comes from* elsewhere, to encourage and strengthen us for good works here.

Wherever that certainty comes from, wherever we anchor our hope—in wildness, beauty, community, or God; in human skill and knowledge and compassion—I believe that we are called to use the strength of it in our own place and time. Those who seek a homeland only in paradise are unlikely to care for their actual homelands in this world. We are not strangers and exiles on earth; we belong here, every neuron and bone. By all means let us yearn and work for a "better country," but let it be *this* country. Let us begin healing the wounds we see all around us, in land and people and in the great fellowship of creatures. What I hear from my children and my students is a cry for *this*worldly hope. I can't offer them a surefire program for easing the world's griefs, but I can show them an orientation of the heart. I can't give them hope as if it were a package neatly wrapped, but I can show them where I have searched for it, and where, in moments of grace, I have found it.

F O U R

W I L D N E S S

HOPE CAUGHT ME BY SURPRISE a couple of weeks ago, when the last snow of winter hit town on the first day of spring. It was a heavy, slashing snow, stinging the skin, driven by a north wind. Because the temperature was near freezing, the flakes clung to everything. A white streak balanced on each telephone wire, each clothesline, on every branch and twig and bud. Many buds had already cracked open after a spell of warm days, so we fretted over the reckless early flowers and eager trees. By noon, snow was piled a foot deep, and more kept falling. The few drivers who ventured out usually wound up spinning their wheels in drifts. Soon even the four-wheelers gave up and the city trucks quit plowing and the streets were abandoned to the storm.

I made the first blemish on our street by going out at dusk for a walk. The light was the color of peaches. The clinging snow draped every bush; even fire hydrants and cars looked jaunty in their gleaming mantles. I peeled back my parka hood to uncover my ears and heard only the muffled crunching of my boots. Now and again a siren wailed, a limb creaked, or wind sizzled through the needles of a pine, but otherwise the city was eerily silent, as though following an evacuation. In an hour I met only three other walkers, each huddled and aloof. The weight of snow had snapped branches and toppled trees onto power lines, leaving our neighborhood without electricity. As I shuffled past the dark houses beneath unlit street lamps, through blocks where nothing moved except the wind, my mood swung from elation toward dismay. The snow began to seem like a frozen burden, like a premonition of glaciers, bearing down from the heedless peach-colored sky. The world had been radiantly simplified, but at the price of smothering our handiwork and maiming trees and driving warm-blooded creatures into hiding.

Drawn by thoughts of family and candles and woodstove, I hastened back to my street, anxious to retreat indoors, into a heated, human space. Nearing our porch, however, I heard a low, steady whinnying from the hemlock beside our front door, and I paused. When I'd first heard that sound, back in January, I had taken it for a distant machine of some sort, a fan belt or furnace blower or pump. But then, listening more closely, I'd recognized it as the single-note gargling of a screech owl. Since then, Ruth and I had been hearing it almost nightly for two months, and one or the other of us would often wake in the small hours to savor this watery song. I didn't expect to hear it during a blizzard, but there it was, persistent as the purr of a brook. I squinted up through slanting snow into the dark boughs of the hemlock and listened as the screech owl, unruffled by the storm, went about its wooing. My mood swung back from dismay toward joy. At length I went indoors, chilled and reassured.

Bird books describe the screech owl's call as a mournful whistling, quavery and tremulous. To Thoreau it sounded "doleful," like "the dark and tearful side of music." At least since Pliny warned that "the Scritch Owl alwayes betokeneth some heavie newes," many have taken the sound for an ill omen. A Cajun forklift driver I worked with at a factory in Louisiana once told me that his trailer was haunted by a "shivering owl." The blasted thing ruined his sleep with its creepy whispering. Had he ever seen it? I asked him. Yes indeed, he'd even had it in the sights of his shotgun, but dared not shoot for fear of bad luck. I knew from his description—a ruddy bird as tall as a robin and twice as big around, with ear tufts and piercing yellow eyes—that he was talking about a screech owl. Indeed, "shiver" comes closer than "screech" to describing its soft, murmuring call.

Every night since first hearing it in January, right on through the blizzard in March and up until the last week of April, as I write these words, I have been listening to my wild neighbor without ever laying eyes on him. A friend tells me I could spy the owl if I probed the hemlock with a flashlight, but I'm content to use my ears. John James Audubon carried a young screech owl in his coat pocket on a journey from Philadelphia to New York, and "it remained generally quiet, fed from the hand, and never attempted to escape." I have no desire to carry this bird in my pocket, to feed it by hand, to capture it on retina or film. Let it remain hidden, a voice calling out of storm and darkness. I hear no ill omen in that sound. On the contrary, I hear in the screech owl's call an energy and yearning and grit that I find immensely encouraging.

Comets were also once thought to be tokens of ill fortune. Anything unusual in the night sky might prophesy war, invasion, plague, the death of a ruler, or some other calamity. The word *disaster*, after all, means ill-starred. We now understand comets to be frozen chunks of debris from the vast cloud of material left over when the sun and planets coalesced out of dust some four billion years ago. They are very old scrap, recycled from earlier generations of stars. Far from being malignant, comets appear to have donated much of our atmosphere and water when they bombarded earth in its early days, perhaps even delivering the carbon compounds necessary for the emergence of life. Though not so numerous these days, they still pass our way, mementos of our origins, snared by the sun into long, looping orbits.

For a month or so, beginning just before the blizzard and continuing well into April, another celebrated comet blazed through the headlines and through our northern skies, moving from Virgo past the Big and Little Dippers to Perseus. Named Hyakutake after the Japanese amateur astronomer who discovered it, the comet followed a path that would bring it around once every eighteen thousand years or so, which means that during its previous visit our ancestors were all still hunters and gatherers, not yet having learned how to plant grains or tame sheep and goats. Compared to the length of my life or yours, eighteen thousand years is a long time; compared to the age of the solar system or universe, it's an eyeblink. In that eyeblink we have learned not only how to sow grains but how to engineer seeds, not only how to tame animals but how to breed new species; we have learned how to transplant trees and hearts, split infinitives and atoms, write sonnets, cure diseases, explore other planets, encode memory on silicon—learned all that and a great deal more, for we are as persistent about inquiring as the screech owl is about wooing.

Much of what we have learned is useful, ingenious, even glorious; but much is also dangerous. In exercising our knowledge, we have made over the planet to suit our needs, and in the process we have done grievous damage. Whether our descendants will still savor life on earth eighteen thousand years from now—and whether millions upon millions of our fellow species will be here to keep them company—depends on whether our wisdom can overtake our knowledge. Whatever our fate, Hyakutake will sweep by on its appointed rounds, indifferent as a blizzard, and that indifference, like the owl's yearning, is a true face of wildness.

When so many of our actions lead to desolation, we should be glad the comets and stars pay us no mind—who'd be willing to answer for the horrors of the twentieth century? To say that the universe in its unfolding takes no heed of our desires is not to say, however, that it is random or crass. The more I learn about the natural world, from science and art and my own senses, the more elegance, order, and splendor I see. When I ponder the way of wild things I do not think of blind chance; I think of the screech owl calling, resourceful and resolute, and of the hemlock shedding snow. I think of maidenhair ferns unfurling and comets tracing their clean curves. I think of seeds and spores and eggs and sperm, those time capsules jammed with souvenirs from past lives and brimming with future lives. I think of images beamed down from the Hubble Space Telescope, showing nebulae giving birth to stars. I think of rafting down the Cache la Poudre with Jesse, working with the river, skirting boulders, reading currents and eddies and waves, apprenticing ourselves to the force of moving water: we do not create that force but merely ride it, by giving the river what the river will not give us—attention and respect and care.

A couple of days after the snowstorm, Ruth called me from her lab at mid-morning, her voice brittle with distress. A colleague who worked in the neighboring lab, she told me, had stopped by earlier to say that he was feeling awful and thought he might go home after finishing a few chores. Usually robust, he looked gray and bent, and everyone had urged him to forget the chores and go right home, or to a doctor, or maybe to the hospital. Somebody would drive him. He'd shrugged aside the offers and gone into his lab, where he'd collapsed a few minutes later, drowned in his own blood from a split aorta. "He was forty-seven," Ruth told me, "and he left four young kids." Later she would explain that the bursting of his blood vessel was programmed into his cells, a case of genetic fate. His children and widow and friends would scarcely be comforted to know that his death was as natural as his birth, as natural as the owl's calling or the comet's return.

On the eve of our wedding, twenty-nine years ago, Ruth and I were out buying presents for the bridesmaids. As I steered into a parking space at an Indianapolis mall, she reached across the seat, put her hand on my forearm, and said quietly, "Wait. Don't get out. I have to lie down for a minute."

"What's the matter?"

"My heart's racing and I need to be still."

My own heart plunged and bucked. "What should I do?"

"Nothing. It'll pass."

She turned, bent her legs, and lay across the front seat with her head in my lap. I stroked her face. With eyes closed, she told me the name of what was happening to her—tachycardia, pulse madly accelerating, the heart's controls gone haywire. She had suffered rheumatic fever at age four, nearly died from it, and this was her heart's echo of that illness. Usually she carried a medicine that would rein it in, but in her excitement over the wedding she had left the pills at home. I smoothed her glistening hair. She was twenty, she was beautiful, she would marry me the next day. How could she ever die?

By and by, Ruth sat up, smoothed her skirt, and looked at me soberly. I felt as though I were meeting her all over again, this time as an adult. Twenty-nine years later, her heart still acts up occasionally, often enough to remind me that she is precious and mortal, and that every cell in our bodies is wild.

Owl, blizzard, comet, heart—all are wild, beyond our will, obedient to their own ways. Clever species that we are, through much of our history we have sought to control wildness, harness it, predict its movements; we have even tried, in our Faustian moments, to abolish it. The same impulse that lifted huge stones into circles thousands of years ago, to measure the cycles of sun and moon and stars, now lofts telescopes and laboratories into orbit. The same impulse that strung weirs across rapids to snare fish now dams whole rivers. The same impulse that tanned buffalo skins and built a fire within the shelter of a tepee also gives us gas furnaces and vinyl siding. We have labored for millennia to superimpose on original nature a secondary one of our own design. As a result of this prolonged effort, those who are most repulsed by wildness, or most afraid of it, can now move into sealed boxes, eat artificial food, shoot their bodies full of drugs, plug themselves into virtual worlds where they are boss.

I'm grateful for a furnace and insulated walls in winter, and for light to read by at night; I'm grateful for the medicine that keeps Ruth's heart in trim, for the plastic lenses that correct my vision, for the bicycle that wheels me around town, for bread and music, for cameras and shovels and shoes. I'm grateful for many, many fruits of human ingenuity.

But I still hanker for the original world, the one that *makes us* rather than the one we make. I hunger for contact with the shaping power that curves the comet's path and fills the owl's throat with song and fashions every flake of snow and carpets the hills with green. It is a prodigal, awful, magnificent power, forever casting new forms into existence, then tearing them apart and starting over.

Crews were busy for days after the blizzard, clearing downed trees from the streets, chain saws roaring. When the snow melted, homeowners trudged across their boggy yards, gathering torn branches and piling them by the curb. Before the city trucks got around to collect those heaps, some of the branches turned rusty pink from redbuds bursting into flower. So for a while the streets seemed to be lined with bonfires, as though for a triumphal procession. But the fires could just as well have been for a funeral procession. Such late snowstorms can wipe out half the population of birds. And in our city alone, hundreds of old trees keeled over or split down the middle. The small woods at the end of our block was a havoc of shattered trunks, bark stripped away to reveal the creamy flesh. Along the sidewalks, the severed redbud limbs went on blooming defiantly, yet no seed would come of those blossoms.

Like the trickster figures who show up in tales the world over, wildness has many guises, but chief among them are creator and destroyer. Coyote and Spider and Hare bring gifts one day and steal them away the next. Even before we hear their stories, we know the truth of them in our bones. Every form that gathers into existence eventually dissolves, every cell, every star—a diamond as surely as a diatom. Each of us is a wave heaved up, holding shape for a while, maybe widening at the waist and thinning on top as the years go by, then sinking again into the primordial waters. Each heart that beats will one day cease.

Knowing this, we have the choice of judging wildness, the very condition of our being, primarily by what it snatches away or by what it gives. We can fix on the brokenness of those redbud limbs, or on their insistent blossoming. We can be most impressed that the owl survives by killing, or that it survives at all, carrying on through sixty million years of storms.

Often in the night, or in grief over a nearby death, I can see nothing of wildness but the destroyer. Most of the time, however, I am struck by the generosity of wild gifts, the fertility of nature, the abundance of creatures and forms constantly rising. Fully aware of loss, and weary of the human veneer spread over the earth, Gerard Manley Hopkins assured us,

> And for all this, nature is never spent;
> There lives the dearest freshness deep down things.

Right now I feel the thrum of freshness, for I write this chapter in spring, while sap rises and green shoots break ground and bright grass licks the air. I keep interrupting work to go outside, stooping over sprouts in the yard, listening to birdsong, moseying through our patch of dirt to see what's new.

One place I check is near the back door, where the hose drips onto a sliced-up block of limestone I rescued from a derelict mill. Last spring I noticed that a little fern had taken root where two saw marks cross in the limestone block, a clutch of feathery green fronds on black stalks as thin as thread. I needed the magnifying glass and the guidebook to identify it as an ebony spleenwort. I had brought dozens of other wild plants in from the woods to our lot, including several ferns, but not this one. I had never seen it in our yard before, nor did I know of any in the yards nearby. Yet somehow the spores had found this good spot, on the shady north side of the house, on damp limestone. It was also a hazardous spot, where feet tromped on their way to the compost bin and the hose dragged. I showed the fern to everyone in the house, so that we could all take care not to crush it. From then on, whenever I used the hose I gave the spleenwort a drink. It seemed too flimsy to survive, yet it held on through summer, pushing tiny green tendrils along the sawmarks in the stone. In fall I covered it with leaves. Today I peel the leaves aside cautiously, as though unwrapping a fragile present—and sure enough, there's the fern, uncurling its newly minted fronds.

Within months after an explosion blew off the top of Mount St. Helens, spewing ash and flattening trees, the first plants and insects reappeared on the slopes, then rodents and birds. Blackened by fire a few years ago, Yellowstone is once more green. Even volcanic islands, sterile heaps of lava flung up from the ocean floor, soon gather life: birds arrive, carrying seeds in their guts and mites in their feathers, and spiders come drifting on the breeze, and uprooted plants ferrying insects come riding the current, and sometimes even mammals wash up, carried on rafts of weeds. It seems not so much that nature abhors a vacuum as that it adores fullness. Yes there is violence as well as freshness "deep down things," as we are reminded by volcanoes and earthquakes and tornados and fires. But so far at least, on our green planet, freshness has won out.

These days when Ruth and Eva and Jesse and I go canoeing on Lake Monroe, a large reservoir near Bloomington, we commonly see a great bird wheeling, its white tail and head gleaming against a backdrop of trees or clouds. As recently as ten years ago there were no bald eagles on the lake, none in southern Indiana, because they had been wiped out by guns and poisons. DDT had been especially hard on the birds, weakening the shells of their eggs so that chicks died before hatching. After DDT was banned and the shooting of eagles was outlawed by the Endangered Spe-

cies Act, state wildlife agents and local volunteers began reintro-
ducing eagles to the lake, using techniques developed by falcon-
ers in the Middle Ages. Eaglets were placed in "hacking boxes"
mounted on towers beside the water, screened from viewing the
humans who climbed up daily to feed them. The feeding continued until the young birds could fly well enough to hunt their own
food. After a couple of years, some of these hand-reared eagles
began rearing their own chicks in the old-fashioned way. This
spring, eagles are nesting in more than a dozen sites around the
lake.

Right now, in hundreds of places across the United States and
other countries, people are at work returning animals and plants
to areas from which they had vanished, reflooding drained wetlands, gathering rare seeds, replanting forests and prairies,
cleaning up rivers, helping endangered species and battered
lands to recover. In Chicago, for example, every weekend volunteers fan out through city parks and forests to plant and weed, restoring patches of the prairie-savanna habitat that once flourished there, on their way toward a goal of reclaiming a hundred
thousand acres. Instead of merely grieving over what has been
lost, these dedicated people, in Chicago and elsewhere, are
working to reverse the devastation. They are reweaving the torn
fabric of life. This worldwide movement of ecological restoration
shows great promise of mending human as well as wild communities. One of the foremost chroniclers of the movement, Stephanie Mills, describes it as "a science of love and altruism." Informed by ecology, inspired by affection, it combines human
intelligence and imagination and sweat with the recuperative
powers of nature to begin healing some of the wounds we ourselves have made.

Except in harsh terrain, such as desert or tundra, the land responds to care, or even to benign neglect. In 1985, as part of that
year's agriculture bill, Congress passed the Conservation Reserve Program, which would pay farmers to take marginal land

out of production and plant it in grass or trees, or let it revegetate on its own. Over the following decade, thirty-six million acres were included in the program, from California to the Carolinas, much of that land on hillsides, in floodplains, or along riverbanks. As these habitats have recovered, soil erosion has declined, water quality has improved, and wildlife has multiplied. Large portions of New England and the Appalachian Mountains are now more heavily wooded than at any time since the early days of European settlement. As the trees have returned, so have bear and beaver and coyote and moose, even wolves and mountain lions, and many other less glamorous creatures.

On the other hand, arid sections of the American West, where overgrazing or salinization have reduced grasslands to dust and rock, will recover slowly, if ever. Even in moist regions, wherever we have kept up our pressure through clear-cutting or careless farming or paving or pollution, habitats are still being degraded and biodiversity is still declining. A recent tally of threatened species published by the World Conservation Union lists more than a thousand mammals, nearly a quarter of all those we know, and more than a thousand birds. Each year's list is longer. We can reverse these trends, as the movement for ecological restoration shows, by living more lightly on the land and by making way for wildness in our yards and parks and forests and farms.

Suppose we quit spraying pesticides and herbicides on our lawns, quit spreading artificial fertilizer, quit mowing, and then filled our yards with native plants. Suppose the poison perfect grass around corporate headquarters were to be replaced with meadows and woods. Suppose every church and school devoted a parcel of ground to a wild garden, where children could meet some of the creatures that belong to their place. Suppose farmers quit plowing to the fence line and planted hedgerows along the perimeters of their fields. Suppose we took seriously the notion of city limits and halted the sprawl of development that is eating up the countryside around every city and town. Suppose we used the dollars taken in by national parks to buy more land for parks. Suppose we never bulldozed another mile of road in national forests and let some of the existing roads revert to woods. Suppose we sowed the margins of our interstate highways with wildflowers from coast to coast.

Nothing keeps us from doing all that, and more, except habit and haste and lack of faith. Faith in what? In our capacity for decent and loving work, in the healing energy of wildness, in the holiness of Creation. One of the reasons many of us keep going back to Thoreau and Muir and Leopold and Carson and others in the American nature writing tradition is because they kept that faith. "Nature is full of genius, full of the divinity; so that not a snowflake escapes its fashioning hand," Thoreau maintains, in opposition to a culture that celebrates only human designs. "One is constantly reminded of the infinite lavishness and fertility of Nature," says Muir. "It is eternally flowing from use to use, beauty to yet higher beauty; and we soon cease to lament waste and death, and rather rejoice and exult in the imperishable, unspendable wealth of the universe."

In seventeenth-century France, a man who entered the Carmelite order at fifty-five and came to be known as Brother Lawrence of the Resurrection told how his spiritual life began at the age of eighteen: "That in the winter, seeing a tree stripped of its leaves, and considering that within a little time the leaves would be renewed, and after that the flowers and fruit appear, he received a high view of the providence and power of God, which has never since been effaced from his soul." Whether or not one attributes the power and providence to God, as Brother Lawrence and Thoreau and Muir did, anyone who stirs abroad in spring, anyone who peers into the fountains of freshness deep down things, cannot help but feel the promise of earth's renewal.

The prime exhibit for the vigor and genius of nature is Creation itself. We cannot get behind the Big Bang, our best current model of how the universe began. That the universe exists at all, that it obeys laws, that those laws have brought forth galaxies and stars and planets and—on one planet, at least—life, and out of life, consciousness, and out of consciousness these words, this breath, is a chain of wonders. I dangle from that chain and hold on tight.

Wildness is the patterning power in this lavish production; it is orderly, extravagant, inventive. Wildness coils the molecules of DNA; it spirals the chambered nautilus and the nebulae; it shapes the whorls on a fingertip, the grain in wood, the planes of cleavage in stone; it regulates the waves breaking on a beach and the beating of a heart; it designs the amoeba's flowing form, the zebra's stripes, the dance of the honeybee; it matches the roundness of nipple and lips and fills the baby with a desire to suck. Wildness destroys, to be sure, recycling whole galaxies, but on balance it creates, bringing new and complex forms into existence; and it has brought forth, in us, a creature capable of gazing back at the source.

Although we have been gazing at our cosmic home for a few million years, we have only begun to fathom the scope and complexity of the universe. As recently as the 1920s, our best guess was that the whole shebang contained one and only one galaxy, the Milky Way. Since then we have kept enlarging our view, at a speed that dizzies the brain. In the winter of 1996, the Hubble Telescope focused for ten days on a point in the sky within the Big Dipper, and the resulting photographs revealed that the universe is far more dense with galaxies than we had previously thought. In fact, the Hubble photos increased our estimate of the number of galaxies fivefold, from ten to fifty billion, and thereby also dramatically increased our estimate for the odds of life having evolved elsewhere.

Measured against all those worlds, all that potential life, what do eagles and owls and ferns matter? Why would it matter if they disappeared, not only from my neighborhood but everywhere?

The most immediate and personal answer is that, if they were gone, I would grieve. Quite aside from their roles in the web of life, they are companions and teachers; they are unique expressions of the beauty that suffuses the whole of Creation. Asking what good are eagles and owls, or ebony spleenworts, or black-footed ferrets, or snaildarters, or any other of our fellow travelers, is like asking what good are brothers and sisters, or children, or friends. Such questions arise only in the absence of love.

We can study wildness, harness it, worship or waste it, but we cannot create it; nor can we extinguish it, in spite of our worst efforts. Life on earth will outlast us, as it has survived ice ages, meteor showers, volcanic eruptions, continental drift. There have been mass extinctions before, and life has always come back. The question is not whether life will go on, with or without us. The question is whether we will continue our reckless use of the earth until we perish, taking innumerable other species down with us, or whether we will work to preserve the intricacy and beauty of our home.

We *can* make peace with the rest of Creation, perhaps more easily than we can make peace with our own kind. Unlike humans, who seethe with resentment over past wrongs, the whales and wolves and rivers and woods hold no grudges. They answer our love with healing. What more joyful and promising work could there be than to help nurture and restore the wild? And for that good work we have a powerful ally in wildness itself.

FIVE

BODY BRIGHT

IT WOULD BE HARD TO IMAGINE a setting less wild than the interior of a subway car rumbling through tunnels beneath city streets. The city happened to be London, but you could not have guessed that from glancing at the passengers. There we sat on plastic benches, forty-two of us by my count, every shade of the human rainbow in every sort of get-up from sari to suit, reading newspapers and books, listening to earphones, clutching bags and briefcases and backpacks, our shod feet shuffling on the rubber floor while lights flickered overhead, wheels groaned below, and a loudspeaker voice called out the names of stations. The nasal drone of that voice might have been playing beneath the streets of any city where English is the common tongue. Although my watch told me it was 9:00 A.M. on July 1, nothing in the Underground revealed whether it was day or night, summer or winter. The smeared windows gave back our own reflections. I was headed to the British Museum, but for all I could see, our subway car might have been a spaceship rocketing to the stars.

Aside from the gleaming metal and glass, every surface was a pastel hue reminiscent of Valentine candies or polyester shirts. Where our ancestors might have painted deer or bison or bear on the walls of their caves, the walls of the car and the stations it rumbled through were plastered with ads for condoms, liquor, movies, banks, weight-loss parlors, record albums, night schools, tourist destinations, soft drinks, air-conditioners, perfume, bluejeans—beckoning images that reminded us of our own cleverness.

We scarcely needed reminding. Weren't we the magicians of this Underground? Except for us, everything within sight or smell or touch had been made by human beings and our machines, and even we ourselves sat muffled in clothes, lathered in cosmetics, hidden behind parcels. Among those forty-two passengers, no doubt many used medicines to regulate their quirky organs; some wore dentures; some flexed artificial joints in hips or knees; perhaps a few hearts ticked to the beat of pacemakers. Certainly there were ears among us that listened with the aid of batteries and eyes that saw through spectacles or contact lenses.

Taking inventory, I noticed that all but one pair of eyes carefully avoided looking into the eyes of any other person.

The bold eyes belonged to a toddler, perhaps a year and a half old, who squirmed in his mother's lap and stared at anyone and everyone, as though he had just been set down among marvels. The utterly clear gaze of those brown eyes swept over me like warm rain. Not content with looking, the child crimped one hand into his mother's blouse and reached out with the other to feel the arms and tug the hair of people sitting nearby. The mother kept pulling him back, apologizing to their neighbors, but he kept groping and staring. In the commotion, a stroller and shopping bag propped against the mother's knee slid to the floor, and when she bent down to retrieve them the child wriggled from her lap and set off toddling among the travelers, peering up into each face as he went, patting legs, babbling a nonstop commentary.

While the mother pursued, the child swayed on down the aisle, and the warmth of his presence thawed the subway glaze. People began murmuring and grinning and stirring wherever he passed, as though restored to life. Even pinstriped businessmen and terminally cool teenagers let loose a smile when he brushed their knees. I suspect that I was not the only one who felt like cheering him on, the uninhibited little animal so curious about his surroundings. But the mother soon caught up, gathered child and stroller and shopping bags, edged toward the door, then hurried off at the next stop, the toddler meanwhile craning around for one last look.

After their departure the glaze quickly hardened again over the passengers. We drew everything tender back inside our shells. The rest of the way to my own stop near the museum, I kept thinking about that baby. We all once dwelt in our bodies with such frank delight. We ran our hands over everything within reach. We sniffed and tasted. We studied buttons and pebbles and bugs as if they were jewels. We turned our cheeks to the wind. We gaped at birds kiting in the sky and froth dancing on water and sunlight flashing through leaves.

> Such richness flowing
> through the branches of summer and into
> the body, carried inward on the five
> rivers!

exclaims Mary Oliver.

Any child is a reminder that the rivers of our senses once ran clear. As we grow older, the rivers may be dammed, diked, silted up, or diverted, but so long as we live they still run, bearing news inward through ears and eyes and nose and mouth and skin. Beneath our grown-up disguises, beneath a crust of duties and abstractions, even beneath the streets of London in a rattling subway car, we are still curious and marveling animals. No matter how much we camouflage or medicate them, our bodies remain wild, bright sparks from the great encompassing wildness, perfectly made for savoring and exploring this sensuous planet; and that is another source of hope. Just as we can help endangered animals and plants to recover and help wounded lands to heal, so we can clean up these rivers that flow into us. And if we restore our senses, they in turn will replenish us.

·   ·   ·

Cities the size of London are not easy places to begin that cleansing, however. I rode escalators and climbed stairs up from the Underground into the bustle and blare of Tottenham Court Road. The breath I drew in tasted like one part air to three parts engine exhaust. The gray sky might have been a scrim. Otherwise, here on the surface, too, nearly everything visible except the crowds had been manufactured: pavement and poles, buildings, buses, and taxis, kiosks heaped with T-shirts and London souvenirs, windows in shops and everything for sale behind the glass. I felt as gray as the sky, my senses numbed by noise and fumes and the crush of people.

Then, as I dodged along the sidewalk, a poster on a news agent's booth caught my eye. It showed a young woman in black bikini, the top undone, a hand cupping a triangle of fabric to each breast; she leaned forward with a grin on her lipsticked mouth and tawny curls tumbled down over her shoulders. Statuesque is the only polite word that comes to mind for describing her shape. It snared me. I paused long enough to see that she was promoting the latest issue of a men's fashion magazine. The caption read: "Bikini or Bust . . . the Body Laid Bare." For a few seconds I gawked, as vulnerable to her paper gaze as I had been to the toddler's real one. Although I did not buy the magazine, I felt stupid for giving in, even momentarily, to this cheap ad. It was as though the woman's shape exactly fit a lock deep within me, opening the door to an old hunger.

Once that door swung open, the women in light summer clothing moving past me on the sidewalks of London kept it open. Their bare arms and legs, their glistening hair, their shining faces seemed all the more vivid against the backdrop of concrete and steel. In the sober light of the British Museum, I fixed my eyes on the antiquities, browsing through the Middle Eastern halls in a vague effort to commune with my Assyrian grandfather and a deliberate effort to forget the bodies laid bare. But there in the first exhibit case I approached were two figurines entitled, accurately enough, "Women Holding Out Their Breasts." One of them sported an elaborate hairdo, the other was painted with designs as if tattooed, and both were naked. Had they worn bikinis they could have been posing for the magazine.

The rest of the morning, in room after room, I kept finding other little statues of women in the same pose, their breasts cupped in their palms. Made from terra-cotta or stone, ranging in date from 5000 to 500 B.C.E., they came from all across the Near East, Anatolia to Babylonia. The labels speculated that the figures might have been fertility charms or amulets to assure safety in childbirth. I could imagine one hanging over the bed, the pallet, or the straw mat as couples made love; I could imagine a woman clutching one as the birth pangs arrived, nine-month fruit of that old, old hunger.

Humans will do almost anything to their bodies, it seems, to heighten their chances of winning a mate: bleach or tan skin, straighten or curl hair, bind feet, flatten heads, stretch lips and ears, cinch waists, inflate biceps and bosoms, tattoo or scarify, pierce and perfume and paint. A good many of these stratagems were on display in the British Museum, among the onlookers as well as in the exhibits. Judging by the size of the human population, the stratagems have been working all too well.

While snared by the woman on the poster, I'd read that her name was Elle, the French word for *she*. The name suited her, for there was something of the archetypal female about her, something primordial, as there was about the figurines in the museum. Images of men rippling with muscles also appeared on pedestals and magazine covers, and they might have been labeled simply *He*, as embodiments of the archetypal male. "The nakedness of woman is the work of God," William Blake declared, and I believe him. The nakedness of man, too. She and He. We ordinary men and women move between these figures as through the charged air between the poles of magnets, pushed and pulled by desires that have been stirring in our kind since the invention of sex.

For the child on the subway, that particular marvel still lay in the future; for a few passengers and museum-goers, perhaps, it lay in the past; but for most of us, most of our lives, the allure of sex is present and potent. Body, body, burning bright. What power framed this fearful symmetry? Like Blake's tiger, humans, too, shimmer with the fierce and magnificent power that lassos the comet and stiffens the fern and guides the owl on its deadly flight. We are wild. Through our bodies, through the ever-flowing channels of our senses, and most vividly through sex, we participate in the energy of Creation. That energy wells up in us like a perennial spring, urging us to ramble and play, to poke about and learn, to seek a mate, join body to body, and carry on with the story.

When I was in high school, the former Marine drill sergeant turned basketball coach who taught health looked aggrieved when he told us that most of what went on inside our skins was beyond our control. "You like to think you're the boss," he would say, "but you're not." Our hearts thumped to their own tunes, he pointed out, just as our glands secreted hormones and our livers filtered toxins and our eyes dilated, just as our cells zipped and unzipped strands of DNA, all without our say-so. "Right now," he told our afternoon class, "you're digesting those baloney sandwiches from lunch whether you want to or not."

For the quiz we learned that something called the autonomic nervous system governs everything from blood flow in our toes to goose bumps on our scalp. "For ten points, define *involuntary*." "For twenty points, compare the human body to a robot." While I wrote my answers, the hair bristled on the back of my neck.

Forbidden in those puritanical times from speaking about the one bodily subject that obsessed us all, our health teacher let us know in his gruff way that certain of our organs and appendages might be unruly at times, even embarrassing, and that strong feelings might wash over us. "Like tides of the sea," he told us, "except less predictable."

As teenagers, we knew without being told that our bodies were swept along by obscure currents. Acne, hot flashes, chills, blood flow and blushes, growing pains in our joints, nightmares looming up from the still waters of sleep—all convinced us that we had lost control. Unable to govern our bodies, we yelled at our parents, we pounded fists into lockers, we teased or dyed our hair, we tortured the engines of cars.

We could remember when life in the body had seemed far simpler, when the world had been a smorgasbord of sensations, all of them delicious. Now suddenly every sensation was edged with danger. The print of a girl's fingers on your elbow, briefly settled there between classes, would burn for hours. A girl might cry all night, so the guys were told, because of the way a boy quirked his lips when he said her name. And when lips opened, no telling what might fly out. Obscenities bred inside there, along with sweet nothings and jokes. Songs would get into our heads and circle like birds of prey. Disastrous odors leaked from every crevice and pore. Dreams lit up our sleep with mad fireworks. In cinemas and drive-ins we watched giant gorillas break out of cages and hairy monsters lumber forth from caves and werewolves howl at the moon, and we knew in our own flesh the truth about these rebellious beasts.

Much of the lore we learned while growing up taught us to be wary of the animal lurking within. We'd all heard of family dogs, as gentle as lambs indoors, that would disappear for a few days into the fields and return with bloody snouts and meat on their breath. Big Foot and Sasquatch, rumored to be shambling through the nearby woods, suggested what we might become if we gave in to our instincts. Stories of satyrs and centaurs bolstered our fear that, however human we might appear above the waist, we were lustful beasts below. In folktales, bears and frogs claimed the heroine's heart only after she broke the spell to reveal that they had been charming princes all along. Beauty might come to love the shaggy Beast in spite of her revulsion, yet he, too, was only redeemed by turning back into human shape.

The very suddenness of these transformations was unsettling. If beasts could so swiftly turn into princes, couldn't princes turn into beasts? Before going on dates, girls were cautioned that no matter how polite a boy might seem in the daylight, he could become savage in the dark. Savage, brutal, bestial, filthy, foul: we learned a litany of scornful names for our animal selves. Boys were cautioned against their own impulses, but also against the wiles of loose girls. "Don't give her that first kiss," our mothers told us, "because you know where kissing leads." Where kissing leads was never spelled out, but we sensed that the werewolf's fur might bristle beneath our own smooth skin, that our teeth might suddenly lengthen into vampire's fangs.

Two bas-reliefs in the Assyrian galleries at the British Museum brought back memories of those teenage anxieties about the body's fierce desires. In one of the stone carvings a protective spirit in the guise of a bearded, winged, and heavily muscled man stands in profile with a goat clamped under his arm; the goat is small and thin by comparison to the man, helpless in his grip, meekly waiting to become supper. In the second carving, an Assyrian king in armor holds a rearing lion at bay with one hand and with the other plunges a sword through the lion's breast. The king is calm, upright, wearing the hint of a smile, while the lion's huge paws flail uselessly and its great mouth sags open in a deathly grimace. In both panels human will triumphs, either by taming the beast or by killing it.

Those twin icons, the good beast and the bad one, the tame and the wild, lay behind the cautionary lore about the body that I learned during my teenage years. One had to choose, it seemed, to become either a docile goat or a dead lion. Only when I went off to college and began reading about cultures other than the ones I'd inherited from Europe and the Middle East did I discover quite different visions of our relations to animals.

In ancient tales from Africa, Australia, China, and India, humans appeal to animals not only for gifts of food but also for guidance on the path of life, and men and women talk freely with monkeys and spiders, birds and snakes, leaping over the chasms between species. In totemic cultures every clan has kinfolk among the animals. The Lakota and Chippewa and Iroquois, the Tlingit and Inuit and many other North American peoples tell stories of humans changing form to become seals or salmon, ravens or coyotes, buffalo or wolves. Wayward, tricky, charged with power, these shape-shifters bring wisdom and spiritual medicine to the human tribe from our nonhuman neighbors. We can only guess what our Paleolithic ancestors meant by painting deer or bison or bear on the roofs of caves, but we cannot mistake the feeling of awe that suffuses those portraits. Although we are clever, these old pictures and tales remind us, we also have much to learn from our fellow creatures, for we are only one tribe in the great circle of life.

This seems to me a more convincing as well as a more hopeful view of our animal nature than the one conveyed to me in high school. The truth is, as teenagers or toddlers or elders, we would be in trouble if we thoroughly tamed or killed off the beast within us, because nothing else keeps us alive. Waking and sleeping, the body goes about its business faithfully, assimilating food and water and sunlight, pumping and circulating, clearing away old cells and making new ones, fighting disease, mending and dreaming. What we call instincts are those enduring habits of the organism that hold us together and keep us going from conception to death. Saint Francis referred to his body as Brother Ass, because it carried him so patiently on life's journey. We each ride our own dutiful beast, however much we may ignore it until injury or illness grabs our attention.

When I began work on this chapter my right thumb was split from a run-in with a chisel. Every bump of that thumb on the space-bar sent pain shooting up my arm. Day by day, as I've added words, the pain has dwindled away, the split has closed, and now fresh skin gleams where the wound used to be. That was a minor cut; I have recovered from worse. In fact, after fifty years, much of my body has been torn apart and reknit. Because of daily wear and tear, in each of us, all the time, countless bruises and scrapes are healing, infections are simmering down, imbalances are being set right. Whether damaged or healthy, all of our cells get replaced every seven years or so. It is as though the body longs to be whole.

A lifetime of study persuaded Carl Jung that the same is true of the psyche, by which he meant the entire mind, conscious and unconscious: "The psychic depths are nature, and nature is creative life. It is true that nature tears down what she has herself built up—yet she builds it once again." Certainly our conscious minds may tip out of kilter—from worry, doubt, hatred, fear—but when that happens, according to Jung, the unconscious mind casts up countervailing images and impulses, thus moving the psyche back toward balance: "The psyche is a self-regulating system that maintains itself in equilibrium as the body does." The fact that most of us are sane most of the time, holding ourselves together while life tugs us in a dozen directions, suggests that Jung is right. The mind, too, longs to be whole.

This parallel between mind and body is precisely what one should expect if these are inward and outward manifestations of a single reality, as I believe they are. Whether we are made up of two substances or only one is a grizzled metaphysical debate, which I do not expect to settle here. In either case, we know that mind and body are intimately linked, that pain and well-being can leap over any gap there may be. Doctors have long known that the state of a patient's feelings, the degree of happiness or grief, hope or despair, can greatly influence the prospects for healing. As both physician and Auschwitz survivor, Viktor Frankl testifies that "the sudden loss of hope and courage can have a deadly effect" by lowering the body's resistance to disease. Following his recovery from cancer, Norman Cousins reports in

Head First on medical research that shows how "the negative emotions—hate, fear, panic, rage, despair, depression, exasperation, frustration" can "produce powerful changes in the body's chemistry, even set the stage for intensified illness," while "the positive emotions—purpose, determination, love, hope, faith, will to live, festivity" can "help activate healing forces in the endocrine and immune systems." Whatever else may be involved in the seemingly miraculous cures performed by faith healers, the faith itself is crucial.

Here, then, are two more reasons to be hopeful: because hope is a healing balm, and because mind and body, against all odds, keep renewing themselves. If you have ever looked at photographs tracing the growth of a fertilized egg into a newborn child, you realize that millions upon millions of things must go exactly right in order for a healthy baby to enter the world; and most of the time, amazingly, they do go right. Once born, we depend on the same organizing genius to keep us going from moment to moment. As in restoring the land, so in restoring ourselves, we can rely on help from wildness.

The body is not endlessly resilient, of course; injuries or disease or the cumulative fraying of old age will eventually break it down. Senility or madness may shatter the mind into pieces so jagged they will never fit back together. In a universe ruled by entropy, where everything slides from order to disorder, this eventual disarray should come as no surprise; the remarkable fact is that an organism can repair and maintain itself for twenty or fifty or ninety years. Life runs counter to entropy, drawing scattered elements and fleeting energies into coherent shapes. The Old English root of *body* means trunk, chest, or cask: thus, a container. You are one of those astounding containers, and so am I, and so is every living thing. We may be temporary, but here we are, each of us a gathered wholeness.

Since we are containers, we must be careful how we fill ourselves. Whatever we take in through our five senses, which Blake called "the chief inlets of Soul," becomes who we are. Try this experiment: Sit beside a freeway for half an hour, listening to the traffic; then sit beside a rocky stream for half an hour, listening to the current. Which sound calms you, feeds you, restores your soul? I expect you will choose the river, not because the mechanical world is evil, but because over millions of years our bodies have been tuned to the sounds of the earth.

Like the London Underground, with its drab concrete and flickering lights and tattered ads, much of the world we have made starves our senses. As we insulate ourselves from wildness, retreating farther and farther inside our boxes, life loses piquancy, variety, delight. So we gamble or drink or jolt ourselves with drugs; we jump from airplanes with parachutes strapped to our backs, or jump from bridges with elastic ropes tied to our ankles; we ride mechanical bucking bulls in bars or drive fast cars or shoot guns, hunting for a lost thrill. We cruise the malls on the lookout for something, anything, to fill the void. Bored with surroundings that we have so thoroughly tamed, we flee into video games, films, pulp novels, shopping channels, the Internet. But all of those efforts eventually pall. As the novelty wears off, once more our senses go numb, so we crank up the speed, the volume, the voltage.

These manufactured sensations pall because they have no depth, no meaning, no *being* apart from ourselves. Again, let me be clear that I am not condemning human works: I spend most of my days in the midst of them. I am only pointing out what a small fraction of the universe they represent. Buildings may be comfortable, machines may be convenient, electronics may be ingenious, but they are never mysterious; they speak of no power, no intelligence, no imagination aside from our own. Like those windows in the subway car, they give back only our own smeared reflections.

No one who has been thoroughly awake to the real universe would swap it for a "virtual" one. Our deepest religious urge, as D. H. Lawrence wrote, is to bring our lives into "direct contact with the elemental life of the cosmos, mountain-life, cloud-life, thunder-life, air-life, earth-life, sun-life. To come into immediate *felt* contact, and so derive energy, power, and a dark sort of joy." Mary Oliver speaks of this craving in a few exultant lines:

> there is still
> somewhere deep within you
> a beast shouting that the earth
> is exactly what it wanted.

No matter how clever our works, they will never satisfy this hunger. Only direct experience of Creation will do. The likeliest way to achieve contact with the life of the cosmos, the likeliest way to recover our senses, is by shutting off our machines and closing our books, climbing out of our tunnels, our cars, our electrified boxes, walking beyond the pavement to actual dirt or rock and opening ourselves to the world we have not made.

Soon after returning from London at the end of July, I visited friends in the Green Mountains of Vermont. One afternoon when they were busy with their jobs, I set off by myself on a hike. The trail led through a meadow where dragonflies dashed and butterflies lolled over the seedheads of grasses, over milkweed and ragweed and hawkweed, over creamy yarrow and purple aster. The borders were boggy but the heart of the meadow was high and dry. I lay for a while on that swell of land, hat shading my eyes against the sun, the smells and sounds and sights pouring through my soul's inlets. The place made me buzz. I plucked a spear of grass and chewed the juicy stem, a sensation I'd loved since long before discovering that Walt Whitman had put it in a poem. I might have stayed there all the afternoon had I not been told by my friends that the South Fork of the Middlebury River lay just up the trail. As a respectable New England river, it would be rocky; and the tug of water sliding over rock will draw me away from almost any other bliss, even from the heart of a meadow.

So after a spell I dusted myself off, picked another stalk of grass for the road, and continued on. Beyond the soggy fringe of the meadow I entered a woods, mostly hemlocks and maples and birches. The trees had been left in peace long enough to grow thick at the waist and gnarly at the roots. The soil underfoot was spongy from the depth of decay. I shuffled knee-deep through cinnamon ferns and skirted mossy hummocks, filling my lungs with moist and loamy air. Before long I heard water, a purring hustle that made my heart glad, and a few more steps carried me to the river. It was rocky for sure, a narrow trough of boulders that shredded the current into dozens of riffles and chutes.

I left my boots and socks on the bank, rolled up my jeans, and waded out to a flat stone in the middle of a rapids. There I sat, enveloped in mist and rushing water-sound. Sunlight broke through the canopy of trees, filling the ripples with scoops of silver and pressing a warm hand against my back. Everywhere I looked, the push of water against rock formed shifty yet durable shapes: a fountain, a braid, a swarm of bubbles like bees, a tinsel of shining strands, a horse's tail, a lacy collar, a curly white wig. I felt like a water-shape myself, flung up on that boulder. Spray licked my face and soaked through my clothes. I started humming, moving up and down the scale until I struck a pitch that sounded in my skull the same as the river. Soon I felt the water flowing through me. Time slowed, circled, came to a halt. There I sat and sat, body laid bare.

Only when the scoops of silver vanished from the ripples and the air grew chill did I realize that the sun had disappeared below the rim of trees. Time resumed its ticking. My friends would be waiting supper for me. So I pried myself loose from the river and hiked back through the shadowy woods, over the darkening meadow, feeling buoyant but full, as though I had already feasted.

Wild surroundings often set me humming. When crickets or frogs or doves are singing, when rain drums on the roof or wind strokes the trees, I hum. I suppose I'm seeking resonance, one vibration of self and world. This old habit seemed less peculiar after I read in Gary Snyder that "the practice of mantra chanting in India, the chanting of seed syllables, is a way to take yourself back to fundamental sound-energy levels. The sense of the universe as fundamentally sound and song begins poetics. They also say in Sanskrit poetics that the original poetry is the sound of running water and the wind in the trees." I'll buy that. What else could have moved us to poetry, back in the dim beginnings of speech, except the earth's own voices?

Such richness carried inward on the five rivers! And it is all a gift of spendthrift nature. Our only task is to wake up, open up, pay attention. God's first act, as recounted in Genesis, is to speak; our first duty is to listen. The eyes may trick us into a sense of mastery, but the ears know better. Sight insists on separation; hearing, like touch or taste or smell, insists on connection. Close your eyes and sound enters you, like juice flowing through the green fuse of the flower, like the surge of dream or desire.

Throughout this book I keep asking, What can we enjoy in abundance, without harming ourselves or our places? Some pleasures are risky to the body—recreational drugs, promiscuous sex, alcohol, tobacco—and some are costly to the earth—flying from the Great Lakes to the Caribbean to get a sun tan, or playing golf on grass kept alive in the Arizona desert, or eating hamburgers harvested from cattle that graze on clear-cuts in the Amazon rain forest. But other pleasures are inexhaustible. "If the doors of perception were cleansed," Blake assures us, "every thing would appear to man as it is, infinite." Sitting on a rock in the midst of a river, studying the sky or the play of light on a tree, tracking the seasons, listening to the wind, turning over pebbles, learning the local plants, watching other animals, walking and talking with someone you love: the riches are there all around us. They require no electricity, no gasoline, no props aside from Creation.

"You must love the crust of the earth on which you dwell more than the sweet crust of any bread or cake," Thoreau advises. "You must be able to extract nutriment out of a sand-heap. You must have so good an appetite as this, else you will live in vain." Wishing to live in earnest, Thoreau took his own advice. In a passage from his journal that would later appear, revised, in *Walden*, he described his reaction to the patterns formed by thawing mud on a railroad embankment: "The earth I tread on is not a dead inert mass. It is a body—has a spirit—is organic—and fluid to the influence of its spirit—and to whatever particle of that spirit is in me."

The particle of spirit in me says yes to that. We are one flesh with the planet and with all our fellow creatures. When the land is ravaged we suffer; when the land flourishes we rejoice. "The problem," says Adrienne Rich, is

> to connect, without hysteria, the pain
> of any one's body with the pain of the body's world.

I believe that's true: we must feel the connection if we are ever to heal either body or world. But I believe the hopeful version to be equally true: our health, our wholeness, our sensual delight are grounded in the beauty and glory of the earth. Since Creation puts on a nonstop show, we may relish the world without exhausting it. And that is the challenge for anyone who seeks genuine hope—to discover, or rediscover, ways of entertaining and sustaining and inspiring ourselves without using up the world.

Our bodies are bright like Blake's tiger, burning with the energy of Creation. They are also bright with curiosity, like the toddling child in the subway car, eager to explore the territory. And they are bright with intelligence. All on their own, they mend and grow, balance and persevere; they yearn to reproduce themselves, and many succeed, passing on through their genes a skein of discoveries. Like all wildness, the body's way is orderly, elegant, complex, and old. It is also fresh, constantly renewing itself, drawing strength from bottomless springs.

SIX

MOUNTAIN
MUSIC II

IF I DREAMED OF HOPE, lying there beside my son during that starry night in the Rockies, I carried no memory of the dream into daylight. I figured there was not nearly enough daylight yet to satisfy Jesse, so I let him sleep while I slithered out of the tent, shoved my stiff legs into cold jeans, and fired up the stove for coffee. So long as he slept we were still at peace.

There was a yeasty tang in the wind, spiced with birdsong from nearby trees and water song from nearby streams. Land slowly parted from air as the sky brightened, revealing the slopes of our valley, the feathery clumps of aspens, and the range of mountains beyond.

Watching the show, I kept remembering scenes from the previous day—the quarrel with Jesse in Big Thompson Canyon, our bucking ride among boulders on the Poudre River, our surprising communion just before sleep. The day had dragged me through so many rough emotions that I could scarcely believe how fresh I felt this morning. It was as though a fist had quit squeezing my heart. Even my gimpy knee had loosened up by the time the coffee water boiled. Whether from dream or mountain air, I sensed a new clarity, in myself and in the world. My struggles with Jesse had convinced me of the need for hope, a lesson I had known but forgotten in my preoccupation with loss. My first thought on waking was that I owed him an accounting of all that gives me courage and joy. Now, on this clear June day in the mountains, I was eager to begin the work.

I wrapped my hands around the steaming mug and gazed at the radiant land. Grasses and pines, ground squirrels and hawks, the very rocks seemed to be bursting with energy. The sight made my pulse rise until I could feel the pressure in my throat. At the top of a clean page in my pocket notebook I wrote "Sources of Hope," and on the line below I wrote "Wildness." The word was a clumsy label for the power I felt in that place and in my hammering heart. Had you asked me to explain it, I could only have pointed.

By and by Jesse stirred, shaking the flimsy tent, and I could not help thinking of the way a cocoon twitches just before the butterfly emerges. What mood would he bring with him, I wondered—the anger of yesterday morning, or the tenderness of last night?

When he did emerge, blond hair tangled into a shaggy mane, he studied the sky with an unreadable expression. After a moment he turned on me a beaming face. "No sign of rain," he said.

"Not yet," I agreed.

He stretched his lanky limbs. "Man, I can't wait to snowshoe."

"Can you wait long enough to eat breakfast?"

Indeed he could. We ate pancakes, drank hot chocolate, washed up, then broke camp and loaded our packs, working in tandem without needing to say who should do what. The little we did say was about the previous day's rafting trip and today's hike into Wild Basin. There was an ease between us that I remembered from when Jesse was little, but that I had rarely felt over the past couple of years. Not knowing how long it would last, I relished every minute.

We drove to the park headquarters to get a camping permit. On the walkway from the parking lot to the backcountry office we met a herd of elk, which languidly moved aside to let us pass and then resumed grazing. On our return with the permit, the herd once again lazily parted before us, hardly missing a bite.

"Do you suppose they're hired to pose for the tourists?" Jesse mused.

"We're tourists," I reminded him.

"Only so long as we stay near pavement and cars."

We stayed on pavement for another few miles, then rolled onto a gravel road that led to the Wild Basin trail head. There we left our rented car, filled our water bottles from an outdoor spigot, and shouldered our packs. It had been a couple of years since I last carried that much weight up a mountain, so I worried how I would fare, even while I enjoyed the heft and balance of the load. A time would come when I could no longer accompany my son on these outings. Legs or back or heart would give out. But not yet, I told myself, heading up the trail, not just yet.

Most of the way to our campsite we hiked within earshot of North St. Vrain Creek, a froth of rushing snowmelt over boulders. The pulse beating in my head merged with the pulse of water in the creek. We made good time, soon leaving the dry lower elevations and rising into areas of patchy snow. Jesse pushed on ahead, driven today by excitement rather than anger. Today I could watch him pulling away without feeling guilt. Now and again I had to stop and catch my breath, unused to such thin air, and he would circle back to wait beside me, uncomplaining. Even when climbing he had plenty of breath for talking, but usually he kept silent, contemplating the trail ahead with a Buddha grin.

Once we stopped long enough to shrug off our packs and take a few swigs of water. Jesse sat facing uphill, forearms across his thighs, humming. I could read on the sweat-darkened back of his T-shirt three lines from the Navajo poet Lucy Tapahonso:

> bless me hills
> this clear golden morning
> for I am passing through again

As I read, a fly settled on Jesse's back and walked across the words, passing through again. Below "Wildness" in my notebook

I wrote "Beauty," which I meant to include the fly, the poem, my son, the mountains, and my own fierce feelings.

All that morning we saw only two other hikers, a pair of wiry young men fitted out in high-tech survival gear on their way down from Thunder Lake. Like us, they had snowshoes tied to their packs. We wouldn't need the snowshoes for another few miles, they told us, but after that it was pure white all the way to the Continental Divide and down the other side.

By noon we found our campsite, in a stand of lodgepole pine just uphill from the boisterous creek. The sparse undergrowth was chiefly myrtle blueberries. Patches of snow two feet deep filled the open spaces, giving way to mud and dry ground near the trunks of trees, where limbs had formed a canopy, and around the bases of sun-warmed boulders. We pitched our tent in the only bare spot large enough to hold it, facing east to catch the dawn. With rough-sawn planks provided by the Park Service to discourage hikers from cutting down trees, we fashioned a pair of benches and laid out our gear. Meanwhile two gray jays flitted from branch to branch overhead, peering down at us and jabbering in their feisty way.

"Sounds like they're giving advice," Jesse said.

"Mainly about where to leave the grub," I said.

Again without needing to divvy up jobs, we soon had our mats and sleeping bags unfurled in the tent, the stove balanced on a flat rock, plastic bottles of eggs and butter plunged into a snowdrift, the food bag strung from a limb beyond the reach of bears, water filtered from the creek and hung in a bag from another tree, wet socks drooping from a clothesline.

"Dad, have you read Hemingway's Nick Adams stories? Especially 'The Big, Two-Hearted River'?"

"Sure."

"You remember the way Nick sets up camp, then looks around, sees everything he needs right where it's supposed to be, and how good he feels?"

"I remember."

"Well that's exactly how I feel." Jesse lay down on a plank, hands clasped behind his head, and stared up through the spires of pines at the sky. "Being out here clears away a lot of confusion," he said.

"For me too."

"Knowing I can carry on my back enough to live for a week in the woods makes me realize how little I really need."

I took out my notebook and wrote "Simplicity" on the page devoted to sources of hope.

The sight of Jesse sprawled on that plank, his face aglow with contentment, made me wish that Ruth were here to see him, to see us, father and son momentarily at peace. And thoughts of Ruth made me think of Eva, way back in Indiana studying birds, and that set me thinking of my mother, who loved to watch the cardinals and bluejays and chickadees jostling at her backyard feeder. And so I traveled through the country of the people I love, remembering them with a sharp joy.

In the notebook I wrote "Family." It would take me months to figure out everything I meant by that word, let alone "Wildness" or "Beauty" or "Simplicity." For now these were talismans for my medicine pouch. They were touchstones that I could turn over and over in my mind as I pondered how to answer Jesse's challenge: Given all that troubles me, about wars and waste and poverty and the devastation of the planet, what keeps me from despair? Where do I find promise of recovery? From what deep springs can we draw strength?

SEVEN

FAMILY

DURING TWO HOT AND HECTIC WEEKS in August, I rushed about trying to meet the needs of everyone close to me. I helped my mother celebrate her eightieth birthday, then helped her choose new linoleum for her kitchen and new strategies for her budget; we spoke about the loneliness of longtime widows; we pored over old photographs, trying to summon up the names of almost-forgotten faces. I wrote to my brother about his winsome baby and to my sister about her irksome job; brother and sister were both feeling trapped by circumstances, and I racked my brain trying to help them figure out how they might wriggle free. Ruth and I spent a day visiting her parents in the Methodist Home, commiserating with them about their ailments, getting them caught up on paperwork and news. Then Jesse wanted to stretch his legs and clear his head before starting college, so he and I went backpacking again, this time in the Smoky Mountains; after we returned, I helped him buy a computer, build a loft for his room, and move into the dormitory. Eva, meanwhile, was getting ready to start graduate school and moving into her own house in our neighborhood, and I helped her by carrying boxes, scrubbing floors, hanging pictures, and running electrical circuits. Morning, noon, and night, Ruth and I talked about nothing except what needed to be done next.

Then one night toward the end of those two weeks I collapsed from heat exhaustion. For several hours, while my temperature perked up near 103 degrees, Ruth tried every method in the first-aid book, and several others besides, in an effort to cool me off. At one point I was lying draped in wet towels in the bathtub, shivering uncontrollably, while she splashed me with cold water from head to foot. Between shivers I was practicing a meditation exercise I'd learned from a Vietnamese Buddhist monk named Thich Nhat Hanh:

> Breathing in, I calm my body.
> Breathing out, I smile.
> Dwelling in the present moment,
> I know this is a wonderful moment.

As I murmured these lines I realized that this *was* a wonderful moment, in spite of the shudders, the fever, the worry we might need to make a midnight run to the emergency room, and I laughed. Ruth thought she had a delirious patient on her hands until I explained to her why it felt so good to be lying there in that icy tub on an August night, worn down by the needs of my kinfolk and by the Midwestern heat, bathed by the hands of the woman I love, knowing I would recover to love and work some more.

In sickness we may forget the body's resilience and damn it as a clumsy contraption. In the grip of natural calamities—earthquake or plague or flood—we may forget the workaday beauty and abundance of Creation. Likewise, if we hear incessantly of war and rarely of peace, if we hear more about crime than kindness, more about divorce than marriage, we may forget how much we need and nourish one another. Grown suspicious of every person we meet, fearing disappointment or disaster, we may withhold ourselves from love and friendship, from any sort of membership, and try going it alone. But that road leads to despair. To find hope, we'll have to travel in company. For just as there is healing in wildness, that perennial spring welling up through body and land and every living thing, so there is healing in community.

Family is the first community that most of us know. When families fall apart, as they are doing now at an unprecedented rate, those who suffer through the breakup often lose faith not only in marriage but in every human bond. If compassion won't reach across the dinner table, how can it reach across the globe? If two or four or seven people who share house and food and even kinship can't get along, what are the prospects for harmony in larger and looser groups, in neighborhoods, cities, or nations? Many of the young people who come to me wondering how to find hope are wary of committing themselves to anyone because they've already been wounded in battles at home.

In the Sanders clan we've made our share of mistakes. We've had our share of turmoil, mainly across generations, including the occasional shouting match, like the one between Jesse and me as we drove through the Big Thompson Canyon in the Rockies. But on the whole we've gotten on well, looking after one another, trading stories and meals, braiding our lives together. Even the quarrels may strengthen our love, the way Jesse's angry words in the mountains set me to writing this book. So I remain hopeful about community, because my own experience of family, in spite of strains, has been filled with grace.

When Eva asked whether I thought she should ever have children, I wanted to shout "Yes!" because Ruth and I have had so much joy from our own children, and because I know Eva will make a superb mother. But Eva was asking for more than a father's hasty vote of confidence. She was asking for a deliberate answer, one that faces honestly the outlook for life in a context of swelling population, dwindling resources, persistent violence, epidemic consumerism, and spiritual drift. Like Jesse, she was asking me whether I believe there are reasons to live in hope not only for ourselves but for our children and grandchildren.

Eva's question became all the more pressing when she and her longtime beau, Matthew Allen, told Ruth and me over supper one evening that they had settled on a wedding date for the following July. I felt a flutter of anxiety and a rush of delight. I gazed at my grown-up daughter, whom I had once held in the palm of my hand, then I gazed at this black-bearded young man, whom we had known since before he needed to shave. With his brooding manner and deep-set eyes, Matt seemed older than Eva. But they were both twenty-three, and they had been circling one another since high school. The circle had gradually drawn them to the center, where they now meant to dwell together forever and ever. It was a sober decision, and, like any marriage vow, a risky one.

"So," said Eva, "do we get the parental blessing, or what?"

Ruth laughed. "You've got mine."

"And how about you, Daddy?" Eva fixed her keen brown eyes on me.

"Heaps of blessings," I answered.

Matt grinned through his beard. "We'll take all we can get."

"We're nervous, I guess," Eva admitted. "Who wouldn't be, these days? But we figured, between you two and Matt's parents, we have more than half a century's worth of evidence that marriage can work."

As we lifted our wineglasses to celebrate, their new engagement rings flashed in the candlelight.

Who wouldn't be nervous, these days, about deciding to get married and perhaps to bring children into the world? The daily news gives us plenty to worry about in the life of families: a mother who drowns her sons by locking them in a car and rolling the car into a lake; a father who rapes his daughter; brothers who murder their parents for the insurance money; junkies who force their kids to run drugs; the estranged husband who stalks his former wife; the celebrity couple who sling insults at one another during their multi-million-dollar custody trial.

It's no wonder that recent commentaries on the American family read like a catalogue of failures and threats. We're warned that marriage is about to disappear, that parents are losing control of their children, that children are growing up without conscience or vision, that grandparents are being shuffled aside, that a legacy of values formerly transmitted from generation to generation is no longer being passed on.

Mesmerized by disaster, we don't often think about the countless families that carry on their work dependably and decently, any more than we think about our cars when they are running well or our bodies when they are fit. It's when the car won't start, when fever lays the body low, when the family breaks down that we pay attention. We are only too aware of the ways in which families can go wrong, can damage children, can twist the lives of husbands and wives, can unsettle communities. How can families go *right*? What are they *for*?

From a biological perspective, the family has evolved to nourish and protect children, and to educate them for survival until they in turn are ready to produce and care for offspring of their own. Many other animals rear their young in families, but none do so over such a long period and none with such elaborate training. We're a slow-developing species, weak and defenseless in our early years. I can remember wondering, as a boy, why my baby brother needed months to learn to crawl, nearly two years to walk, when the ponies we raised on our Ohio farm could romp about within minutes of birth. I'm still amazed at the speed with which most other animals mature. From my desk I can hear the newly hatched cardinals and robins in our yard haranguing their parents for grub, and yet in a few days they will be fledglings swooping about and feeding themselves.

Slow to develop physically, we also take a long time to acquire the skills necessary for survival. By comparison with other animals, we depend far less on instinct, far more on learning. Much of our education consists of finding out how to get along with other people, inside and outside the family, how to talk with them, work with them, bargain and joke and play with them, because we're a social species, needing the cooperation of our fellows in order to secure food and shelter, to decipher the patterns of nature, to defend ourselves against predators and sickness and rival humans, to ponder the meaning of life and the mystery of death.

Needing so much knowledge, we're also a species that has valued its elders, those with the longest memories, those who carry the lore and wisdom of the tribe. The oldest burial sites of our human ancestors include the bones of people crippled by disease and gnarled by age, people who could have survived only through the care of younger companions. We might attribute that care to loyalty and compassion, but these sentiments have clear evolutionary benefits, since they assure the passing on of knowledge. The human clans that neglected their elders, like those that neglected their children, soon perished.

Watching Eva and Jesse grow up, I've been astounded by the force of their curiosity and the swiftness of their learning, but I've been equally astounded to realize how much they must know in order to function as adults in our complex society. From balancing on their legs to balancing equations, from tying their shoes to paying their taxes, from naming the parts of the world to programming computers, they've learned a staggering amount. Even in technologically simpler societies, boys don't become men, girls don't become women, until they've studied the ways of adults for a dozen years or more. Such education has always come in part from outside the family, from elders and teachers, from the men's lodge or the women's lodge, from neighbor children, from priests and strangers and storytellers and—over the past few hundred years—from books. Yet no matter how much instruction comes from outside, the family is the arena where learning begins, where knowledge may be tested and mistakes be made, where the hard business of becoming human may be safely practiced.

The family, then, is not a sanctuary cut off from the rest of society, not a secluded preserve, but a training ground for life in community, in village or clan or tribe. If there is to be a vigorous community for children to join, the family must also provide, in Gary Snyder's phrase, "the Practice Hall" for adults as well, a place where men and women perform the ceremonies of mutual aid, amuse and challenge one another, share comfort and love. By all these measures, a good family is one that encourages the full flowering of parents; that cherishes grandparents as carriers of wisdom; that nourishes children in body and mind and soul, and prepares them to enter the world as responsible and competent adults.

On a Saturday morning in late September, a month after my bout with heat exhaustion, Eva came over to help Ruth make pies for a supper that we would share in the evening with Matt's family, the Allens. Mincemeat, apple, pecan. I was up on the roof emptying leaves from the gutters, but I kept making excuses to climb down the ladder and visit the kitchen, where I breathed in the luscious smells and listened to the women talk. One minute they were talking about genetics, the next minute about politics, and the next about wedding dresses. Eva's hands moved in harmony with Ruth's, cutting fruit, rolling out dough, scattering spices, crimping the edges of crusts.

I broke in to ask, "Do you need me to test any of that filling?"

"Here," said Ruth, lifting a spoonful from a mixing bowl, "let's see what the expert thinks of our mincemeat."

I rolled the fruity sweetness in my mouth. "Not bad," I said, "but I'll need another bite to make sure."

"One more spoonful, then go finish your gutters and let us finish our pies."

I left the kitchen reluctantly. "Remember to listen for my yell, in case I fall off the roof."

"Just don't break any legs before July," Eva warned. "You've got to walk me down the aisle."

Back on the roof, scooping hemlock needles and maple leaves from the gutters, I felt no dizziness from the height, from the clouds scudding by, from the whirl of chimney swifts overhead, but I did feel dizzy over the prospect of walking Eva down the aisle.

Later that morning, the pies all baked, Eva took off to scour yard sales in search of chairs for her newly rented house. Meanwhile, Ruth and I went over to my mother's house to do some small repairs. We fixed a storm door, replaced a rubber gasket on the garage door, changed a light switch, installed a bathroom exhaust fan. While Ruth and I traded hammers, screwdrivers, and pliers, Mother was busy repotting plants—lilies, geraniums, impatiens, azaleas. She would be leaving soon for a trip to Ireland, and she wanted to ease our chore of watering her plants while she was gone. As we gathered our tools, Mother gave me a bag of roasted seeds from a pumpkin she had cleaned. "Share them with Jesse," she told me, and I promised that I would.

What values and behaviors should the family teach if it is to be a training ground for life in community? That all depends on what sort of community we desire. For my part, I wish to live in a community that is peaceful, that cares for the weak and the poor, that welcomes the immense variety of humankind, that fosters the health and happiness and full development of all its members, young and old, male and female. I wish to live in a community that is beautiful, that encourages good work and discourages everything hasty or shoddy. I wish to live in a community that acknowledges the holiness of Creation by conserving the land and by respecting the creatures that share the land with us. I wish to live in a community that recognizes its links to the larger world yet also meets many of its own needs, especially for food and entertainment, and that has a modest sense of what those needs are. I wish to live in a community inhabited by citizens rather than consumers, public-minded people who honor the richness of our shared life by supporting libraries and museums and schools, and by planning for the common good. I wish to live in a community that has a keen awareness of its own history, one that values continuity as well as innovation and aspires to leave a wholesome place for others to enjoy, undiminished, far into the future.

That vexed phrase "family values" often serves as shorthand for a political agenda that is never spelled out. I have my own agenda, which is why I've sketched this vision of a desirable community. The family values that I embrace are the habits of heart and mind essential for creating and maintaining such a community, and among these are generosity and fidelity and mercy, a sympathetic imagination, a deep and abiding concern for others, a delight in nature and human company and all forms of beauty, a passion for justice, a sense of restraint and a sense of humor, a relish for skillful work, a willingness to negotiate differences, a readiness for cooperation and affection. I don't pretend that we always live up to those values in my own family, but we aspire to do so.

While the family is not the only place where we might acquire such habits, it is the primary one. And above all it is the place where we are most likely to learn the meaning of love. In using that tricky word, I note Wendell Berry's distinction between the *feeling* of love, which may be no more than a warm and fuzzy glow, and the *practice* of love, which involves "trust, patience, respect, mutual help, forgiveness," and other demanding virtues. If children and adults emerge from a household bearing those habits of heart and mind, I would declare that family a success, a blessing to its neighbors and its place.

I am all too aware of the distance between these ideals, for community and family and individual character, and the reality we meet in contemporary America. In most of our households, real income has been stagnant or declining for twenty years, despite the fact that more women and more mothers of young children are employed outside the home than ever before. A third of all jobs carry no health insurance, and that percentage is increasing. The rate of divorce is also increasing, along with the rates of homicide and suicide among children; and the rate of domestic violence continues to be appallingly high. Over the course of a year, children spend on average about twice as many hours watching television as attending school. Today, sixty percent of our families are headed by single parents, and half of those parents have never been married. Every day, roughly two million children return from elementary or middle school to a home where there is no adult to look after them for many hours. More of our children than ever before *have* no homes, more families are living on the streets, more people of all ages dwell in poverty.

We needn't harken back to the supposedly halcyon days of the "nuclear family" (a label that summoned up for me, as a child in the1950s, the specter of radioactive homes) in order to recognize that our social fabric is coming unraveled. I don't pretend to know the reasons for this unraveling, but I can't help noticing that our economic system is hostile to virtually all of the values I listed earlier. Our economy rewards competition rather than co-operation, aggression rather than compassion, greed rather than generosity, haste rather than care. Our jobs commonly separate work and home, demand longer and longer hours from employees, and punish those who take time out for child-rearing. When a corporate CEO is paid a hundred times as much as a school-teacher or a factory worker, and when the richest one percent of Americans earn as much as the poorest forty percent, how does one teach a child to believe in equity and justice? When success is measured only by quarterly reports, how does one teach patience? When corporations close plants and move their operations overseas or to rival states in order to boost their profits, how is one to teach loyalty? How does one teach modesty or restraint when advertising promotes instant gratification as the goal of

life, and the media celebrate excess and arrogance? When entre-
preneurs treat every square inch of the planet as raw material,
how does one teach a conserving love for the earth?

We are the richest nation on earth, yet study after study shows
that the greatest threat to American families is poverty. Certainly, individuals and families and entire communities act in
ways that contribute to their impoverishment, and insofar as we
can identify such harmful ways we should do everything we can
to help those who are struggling to overcome them. But it is hypocritical to exhort young people to abstain from sex when our
merchants rely on sex to sell their products. It is hypocritical to
demand from the poor a higher level of moral behavior than ce-
lebrities or executives or stockbrokers or politicians consistently
demonstrate. It is dishonest to exhort the unemployed to try
harder when they have no marketable skills and no prospects of
acquiring such skills. It is dishonest to blame the poor for being
poor when millions of those who work full-time cannot earn a living wage. The fact is that our economy has less and less use for
more and more people, and most of those discarded people know
and bitterly resent this.

Finished for the moment with repairs at my mother's house,
Ruth and I went home for lunch. The lingering fragrance of pies
gave way to the smell of sesame oil as Ruth stir-fried vegetables.
While I was setting the table, Jesse showed up, a refugee from the
bland fare of the dormitory cafeteria, so I set an extra place.

"You're just the man I wanted to see," I told him over our
steaming plates.

"Uh, oh," Jesse said. "That sounds like work."

"It'll be good for you. Stretch those big muscles of yours. We're
going out to the Allens' this afternoon to help Don cut up some
trees that washed onto his field down by the creek. Matt will be
there, too."

"Count me in," said Jesse.

"Charlene and Eva and I are going to talk about the wedding," Ruth added.

"And we're going to stay for supper," I said. "With three kinds of pie."

"I'll pass on the wedding talk," Jesse said, "but supper sounds great."

We loaded the car with chain saw, gas can, splitting maul, wedges, and gloves. Then we drove beyond the sprawling fringe of town into the hills bordering Clear Creek, where Matt's parents, Don and Charlene, had recently built a house. As we rolled down the gravel drive, we could see Matt and Eva in the open door of the garage, bending over four ladder-back chairs. Two young bird dogs romped in circles around them, begging to play fetch-the-stick. Don and Charlene sat on the front steps, surveying their new yard. We climbed out of our car, greeted the dogs, greeted the Allens. Eva wanted to know what we thought of the chairs, which she had bought at a yard sale. I examined them one by one. The seats were gone, the joints were loose, and the finish was a patchwork of grimy shellac.

"They'll be gorgeous after you fix them up," I said. "Refinish them, reglue them, weave some new seats, and they'll be strong and balanced and light."

"They're like ours at home, aren't they?" Eva asked.

"Just like ours," Ruth agreed.

"Did yours ever look that bad?" Matt asked with a note of skepticism.

"Worse," Ruth said. "One of them came to us as a bundle of sticks."

"So where do we start?" Eva asked.

The four parents spoke at once, and then we laughed and took our turns. Between the Allens and the Sanderses, it turned out, we possessed all the knowledge and tools needed for restoring ladder-back chairs. With family help and plenty of elbow grease, Eva and Matt would turn these rickety yard-sale discards into sturdy seats for the new household they were about to form. Eva wanted to begin right away, figuring she could talk about the wedding and strip chairs at the same time, so she and Ruth and Charlene went off to gather steel wool, alcohol, and glue.

The four men, meanwhile, loaded saws and wedges and mauls into Don's truck. Jesse and Matt climbed in back along with the bird dogs, and Don and I climbed into the cab; then we jounced down the hill and across a stubbled field to the bank of the creek, where summer floods had flung a snarl of driftwood. The chain saw roared on the first pull and for a while I did the cutting, Jesse did the carrying, Don and Matt did the splitting. We soon peeled off our jackets and sweated along in T-shirts and jeans and boots. We worked quickly through most of the pile of wood, mainly beech and hickory, then took a rest before tackling the fattest log. Bare of bark, it was from a tree that had been dead quite a while, but the wood seemed sound. Neither Don nor I could tell from the shape alone what it was, although we both were guessing oak.

The dogs bounced around our legs, nuzzling us, and eagerly chased any stick we cared to throw. The creek slid by, dappled with scarlet reflections on this September afternoon, and crows caucused in the tops of sycamores that leaned toward one another from opposite banks. Matt and Jesse also leaned together, sitting on the tailgate of the truck and gabbing away about music, and I thought how much they would be able to give one another as brothers-in-law. Don and I talked about carpentry and cosmology.

Before our sweat cooled we started on the big log. This time Jesse handled the saw, Matt lugged the cut sections, Don and I swung the splitting mauls. The first cut revealed the wood to be red oak, long dead but still firm. Each round of log split with a solid *thunk*, usually on the first blow.

After another hour or so of labor, interrupted now and again for wisecracks and water, we had cut and split all but the stump of the great log, with its tangle of naked roots. What the creek had flung in one casual motion onto the bank, we flung in several hundred pieces into the truck. The shock absorbers groaned under the load as we drove back up the hill to the Allen house, then on into town to the Sanders house, where we unloaded the wood, stacked it on a platform beside the compost bins in the backyard, and covered it with a blue tarp. Then we retraced our path into the country, where the women had already stripped two of the ladder-back chairs, and where we ate all three pies.

Now, whenever I light a fire in our woodstove I think about cutting up the drift logs with Jesse and Matt and Don, about Eva restoring her chairs with help from Ruth and Charlene. I think about our expanding family in the midst of family, just as each of you, reading this, dwells in your own force field of kinship and responsibility and affection. I use the physics metaphor deliberately, because life in family feels to me like a constant giving and receiving of energies, with each member bound by memory and thought and emotion to all the others. We exchange labor and sympathy, we teach and learn, we nourish and nag, without calculating who owes what to whom. When any one in the family hurts, everyone aches; when any one exults, everyone celebrates.

Although Ruth and Eva and Jesse are at the center of my own force field, the influences of family as I experience them reach out beyond those who've shared a house with me, beyond kinfolk related to me by marriage or blood, to include those friends and neighbors and ancestors whom I carry in mind as vital presences. I act, always, before a cloud of witnesses. There is no sharp outer boundary to this set of people whose needs and moods tug at me, but only a gradual tapering away of their influence the farther they are from my emotional center.

Just as I am bound in kinship beyond the limits of my knowing, so any family is bound to other families, to neighborhoods, to schools and libraries, to places of work and places of worship, to shops and clubs and hospitals and parks, to local communities and the larger society. If that society is troubled, no walls, no stretch of lawn, no insurance policy, no fervent faith will keep the troubles out. There are more than enough troubles in contemporary America to unsettle any household: poverty, infidelity, illiteracy, racial strife, drug addiction, alcoholism, unemployment, mayhem in the media and on the streets.

In spite of these troubles, even in the most hostile and dangerous settings, families endure. As the biologist E. O. Wilson reminds us, "The family, taking either a nuclear or extended form, has rebounded from countless episodes of stress in many societies throughout history." But even if families endure, will they be able to carry on as centers for education and care? Will they be able to nurse children along safely from infancy to responsible adulthood? Will they make room for grandparents and preserve the wisdom of elders? Will they serve as training grounds for life in community?

None of us can guarantee that the answer to those questions will be yes, but all of us can help to make that answer more likely for ourselves and for others. If we are intent on strengthening families, we could push for changes in the job culture, such as flexible scheduling and child care at the work site and paternity as well as maternity leave, changes that allow parents more time with their children and couples more time together. We could turn off our televisions, and leave them off, unless there's a worthy reason for turning them on. We could denounce those broadcasters and filmmakers and advertisers who cheapen life. We could work to see that all pregnant women, all children, indeed all Americans receive decent health care. Instead of blaming the poor for their poverty, we could make sure that they receive training and jobs. We could worry less about who lives with whom, and worry more about the quality of their lives together.

Those of us who have more than we need, of money and possessions, could choose to own fewer things and spend less. We could resist the calls of consumerism, and share some of our abundance with families who have little. Those of us who hold jobs could bear in mind, always, the impact of our work on the world, for the present and for the future. Those of us who are retired could choose to stay near our children and grandchildren, or in towns and cities where we have long-standing friendships, rather than shuffling off to recreational villas; wherever we live, we could invest our wisdom, talents, and time in the community.

While acknowledging that it takes a village to raise a child, we must remember that it takes citizens to make a village. If we are intent on strengthening families, we could help to restore our cities and towns and neighborhoods. We could defend those institutions and programs that we can only create *as citizens*, which means defending the good that we can do together through government. We could speak up for the commonwealth, for the land and water and air and our fellow creatures; we could speak up for future generations and their right to inherit an undamaged planet. While holding our public officials, our legislators and regulators, our judges and teachers accountable for their work, we should also give them humane conditions for carrying on that work, and we should hold ourselves accountable for the services we require of them.

There is no shortage of work to be done, and much of it must be done against the grain of our commercial culture. But the family is much older than television or advertising or global corporations, and I suspect it is more durable. The root meaning of the word *family* is household, a gathering of people who take shelter together. No matter how troubled our households, we're going to keep on taking shelter together because we need one another; we need protection when young, help when old; we need guidance and companionship and affection our whole lives long; we need a kindly place where we can fall sick of heat exhaustion or celebrate a wedding or share bread. In the struggle between a destructive, reckless, shallow culture and these ancient human needs, I place my faith in the family.

EIGHT

FIDELITY

WHEN I WAS COURTING RUTH I memorized a bundle of poems, to make sure I'd have somebody else's artful words handy whenever my own words failed. One of the sure signs that I had found the right woman was that Ruth could listen with a straight face while I reeled out a verse, as though it was the most normal thing in the world. The other women I knew in those days would have started heading for the door, or rolling on the floor, if I'd lapsed into poetry.

Among the first poems I learned for wooing purposes was the Shakespeare sonnet that begins,

> Let me not to the marriage of true minds
> Admit impediments. Love is not love
> Which alters when it alteration finds . . .

Even as I recited those lines, I wondered how we could tell for certain whether our minds were true. Were we in love for life, or merely infatuated? Could the dizzy attraction I felt toward Ruth ever be dulled by alterations, in her or in me? Could we grow weary of one another, the way some older couples we knew seemed to have grown stodgy and stale? Spooked by those questions, I reserved Shakespeare for solemn occasions, and opted most often for less worrisome lyrics by the likes of Donne and Yeats and Neruda and Frost.

Did the poems help to win Ruth over? Maybe a little, she admits when I put the question to her at breakfast.

"Even the one about the marriage of true minds?"

"How does it go?" she asks.

I launch into the sonnet over our cooling bagels, get stuck halfway through, then have to go look it up to finish the last lines:

> If this be error and upon me proved,
> I never writ nor no man ever loved.

Ruth smiles. "Oh, that one! Sure, I liked sly old Shakespeare too."

Whatever the effect of the poems, she did agree to marry me, and since then all the evidence has suggested that we're in love for life. After thirty years of marriage, and quite a few alterations, I still feel attracted to her, maybe not so dizzily, but more steadily and powerfully than ever. It's that *more* I want to speak about here—the depth of feeling and richness of meaning and strength of purpose that only emerge from long commitment. Although I open with the example of marriage, I'm also thinking about other sustained commitments—to friends, to work, to place, to causes and concerns. We all try out a lot of enthusiasms, chase a lot of rabbits hither and yon, but what we stick with after the infatuation wears off is what defines our lives.

I don't mean habit. I don't mean trudging along in a rut. I mean actively choosing, over and over, to stay on a path, to abide in a relationship, to answer a call. The sort of commitment I have in mind is compounded of stubbornness, affection, and wonder. My shorthand term for it is *fidelity*, by which I mean not only the honoring of marriage vows, if you happen to be married, but keeping faith with anyone or anything that claims your love.

Fidelity is not a virtue to brag about, but a native impulse, like curiosity. I see it in Jesse and Eva, in my students, and in many other young people—a yearning to find a person, an idea, a vocation, a cause to embrace with a whole heart. What holds them back is the fear they'll find nothing worthy of their dedication; the fear of being disappointed, deceived, or hurt; the fear of being mocked as fools for showing loyalty in a culture that celebrates fickleness and fashion. They look around and see aimless mobility, broken promises, shifting allegiances, and the frenzied pursuit of novelty. They hear voices urging them to avoid entanglements, keep their options open, always look for something sweeter. Against that clamor for change, I wish to celebrate our capacity for steadiness and devotion. Here is an antidote to drift. Here, in fidelity, is another source of healing and hope, freely available to all, like wildness or the body's own resilience.

A while ago Jesse and I went to a performance by a jazz band from South Africa, fifteen young men and one young woman, all of them visiting America for the first time. Their conductor was a round, restless, exuberant trumpeter named Johnny Mekoa who had come to the university where I teach on a Fulbright Scholarship some years earlier to earn a degree in music, had then gone back to South Africa to start a school, and had now returned with his students to show the fruits of his work.

The fruits were delicious. The band played American and African pieces by turns, riding hot rhythms back and forth across the ocean, and between numbers Mekoa praised his young musicians. Two years earlier most of them had never held an instrument, never read a line of music. Some of them had been living in squatter camps, some had been living in the streets. Yet here they were, after only two years of practice, cooking up spicy jazz for a wildly appreciative audience in this music-loving place.

Now and again during the program I glanced at Jesse, who sat with some of his friends down the row from me. The look on his face was rapt, washed clean, shining, the same look he had while churning through whitewater on the Cache la Poudre River.

As Mekoa spoke he kept bowing to his former teachers in the audience. He told how in the grim old days of apartheid he had learned to play jazz by listening to smuggled records. When the walls of apartheid came tumbling down, he itched to give up his job as an optician and go study trumpet in the land where jazz was invented. His wife, a nurse, said go ahead; she would hold down the fort while he was gone. So he traveled to Indiana; he worked night and day, the sooner to finish his degree and return home to his wife; then he went back to South Africa eager to start his own school. Music would help mend the torn fabric of his bedeviled and beloved country. "Why should we fight, if we can dance together?"

Supporters in America and England sent him sheet music and instruments, and he set up shop in an abandoned warehouse. He went the rounds of the poor neighborhoods, found young people who wanted to learn, and started giving lessons. He found other teachers, one for keyboard and one for saxophone. He scrounged up money from businesses, foundations, and private donors, and from the amazing new government headed by Nelson Mandela. Soon music began wafting from that disused warehouse. With his first students he gave concerts for street children, and the urchins whose eyes shone the brightest he recruited for his school.

"When I looked at these children," he told us, "I knew there were artists among them. I could see it in their faces."

In the question period following the concert, Jesse asked how you teach someone to improvise. I knew the question came from Jesse's own efforts on the guitar.

Mekoa pressed the trumpet to his chest. "You improvise with your ear and your heart. There are no wrong notes. Whatever you feel moved to play, play it. When you hear how it sounds, then you can decide whether to play it so again."

I came away feeling that Mekoa's many strands of devotion—to jazz, to the trumpet, to his wife, to his homeland and his students, to the composers and teachers and performers whose work he is passing on, to audiences, to the future of South Africa—are braided together into a single vocation. He was called to make music, share it, teach it, pass it on; he was called, and he answered yes. He keeps on saying yes with body and soul. Jesse could see, we all could see, that here is a man who has found a purpose, a man who knows why he is alive.

I prize integrity of purpose even when the fruits of it set my teeth on edge. Recently a local woman wrote to the newspaper to say that she was retiring from her role as gadfly to the school board. You could almost hear a sigh of relief spreading across town as people read the announcement. For longer than the twenty-five years Ruth and I have lived in Bloomington, this woman has shown up at every school board meeting, followed every debate, and challenged every proposal by demanding a return to basics. Basics will save us, she declares. Basics will restore morals to our wayward society. Basics will keep children afloat in the choppy seas of life. Reading and writing and arithmetic were good enough for our ancestors who built this great country, yet these subjects have been squeezed out of our schools by all this rubbish about diversity and drugs and self-esteem and sex. Teaching about sex is the worst folly, she maintains, because it only gives young people lewd ideas.

This woman had telephoned me once to complain that in a book of mine about the Indiana limestone quarries I had put swear words in the mouth of a retired mill worker.

"I didn't put them there, ma'am," I replied. "I wrote a few of them down after they came pouring out, and the mildest ones at that."

"You're corrupting our youth," she told me.

"By suggesting that some of their elders occasionally say 'hell' and 'damn'?"

"You're corrupting our youth," she repeated.

She could have sent a tape recording to deliver her message to the school board, it was that predictable, but instead she delivered it in person. Neither rain nor snow nor dark of night kept her from showing up. Ridicule would not silence her. Why did she keep coming to meetings, keep reading interminable reports, keep raising objections? She had no children in school. She wasn't running for office. She wasn't anybody's paid lobbyist. You might figure she just liked to hear herself talk, or maybe she craved an audience. But the audience was usually hostile, and the words burst from her with a note of exasperation, as though she would much rather not have had to say them. No, there was nothing of the show-off about her. Then why her persistence? I think she was simply determined to be a good citizen and to stand up for her convictions. In doing so, she made the rest of us think harder about our own convictions, made us a bit more honest. And isn't that how democracy is supposed to work, with informed citizens debating the issues vital to their common life? I hardly ever agreed with her views, but I admired her tenacity and grit.

A cause needn't be grand, it needn't impress a crowd, to be worthy of our commitment. I knew a man, a lifelong Quaker, who visited prisoners in our county jail, week in and week out, for decades. He would write letters for them, carry messages for them, fetch them clothing or books. But mainly he just offered himself, a very tall and spare and gentle man, with a full shock of white hair in his later years and a rumbling voice that never wasted a word. He didn't ask whether the prisoners were innocent or guilty of the charges that had landed them in jail. All that mattered was that they were in trouble. He didn't preach to them, didn't pick and choose between the likable and the nasty, didn't look for any return on his time. Nor did he call attention to his kindness; I had known him for several years before I found out about his visits to the jail. Why did he go spend time with outcasts, every week without fail, when he could have been golfing or shopping or watching TV? "I go," he told me once, "in case everyone else has given up on them. I never give up."

Never giving up is a trait we honor in athletes, in soldiers, in climbers marooned by avalanches, in survivors of shipwreck, in patients recovering from severe injuries. If you struggle bravely against overwhelming odds, you're liable to wind up on the evening news. A fireman rescues three children from a burning house, then goes back inside a fourth time to rescue the dog. A childless washerwoman in the deep South, who never dreamed of going to college herself, lives modestly and saves her pennies and in old age donates everything she's saved, over a hundred thousand dollars, for university scholarships. A pilot flies his flimsy plane through a blizzard, searching for a pickup truck in which a woman is trapped; gliding and banking through a whirl of white, he catches signals from her cellular phone, ever so faint; the snow blinds him, the wind tosses him around, his fuel runs low, but he circles and circles, homing in on that faint signal; then just before dark he spies the truck, radios the position to a helicopter crew, and the woman is saved. What kept him searching? "I hadn't found her yet," he tells the camera. "I don't quit so long as I have gas."

Striking examples of perseverance catch our eye, and rightly so. But in less flashy, less newsworthy forms, fidelity to a mission or a person or an occupation shows up in countless lives all around us, all the time. It shows up in parents who will not quit loving their son no matter how much trouble he causes, in parents who will not quit loving their daughter even after she dyes her hair purple and tattoos her belly and runs off with a rock band. It shows up in couples who choose to mend their marriages instead of filing for divorce. It shows up in farmers who stick to their land through droughts and hailstorms and floods. It shows up in community organizers who struggle year after year for justice, in advocates for the homeless and the elderly, in volunteers at the hospital or library or women's shelter or soup kitchen. It shows up in the unsung people everywhere who do their jobs well, not because a supervisor is watching or because they are paid gobs of money but because they know their work matters.

When Jesse was in sixth grade, early in the school year, his teacher was diagnosed as having breast cancer. She gathered the children and told them frankly about the disease, about the surgery and therapy she would be undergoing, and about her hopes for recovery. Jesse came home deeply impressed that she had trusted them with her news. Before going to the hospital, she laid out lesson plans for the teacher who would be replacing her. Although she could have stayed home for the rest of the year on medical leave while the substitute handled her class, as soon as she healed from the mastectomy she began going in to school one afternoon a week, then two, then a full day, then two days and three, to read with the children and talk with them and see how they were getting on. When a parent worried aloud that she might be risking her health for the sake of the children, the teacher scoffed, "Oh, heavens no! They're my best medicine." Besides, these children would only be in sixth grade once, and she meant to help them all she could while she had the chance. The therapy must have worked, because seven years later she's going strong. When Ruth and I see her around town, she always asks about Jesse. Is he still so funny, so bright, so excited about learning? Yes he is, we tell her, and she beams.

I have a friend who builds houses Monday through Friday for people who can pay him and then builds other houses on Saturday, with Habitat for Humanity, for people who can't pay him. I have another friend who bought land that had been stripped of topsoil by bad farming, and who is slowly turning those battered acres into a wildlife sanctuary by halting erosion and spreading manure and planting trees. A neighbor of ours who comes from an immigrant family makes herself available night and day to international students and their families, unriddling for them the puzzles of living in this new place. Other neighbors coach soccer teams, visit the sick, give rides to the housebound, go door to door raising funds for charity, tutor dropouts, teach adults to read; and they do these things not just for a month or a season but for years.

There's a man in our town who has been fighting the U.S. Forest Service for two decades, trying to persuade them to quit clear-cutting, quit selling timber at a loss, quit breaking their own rules in the Hoosier National Forest. All the while, those who make money from tearing up the woods call for more cutting, more road-building, more board feet. This man makes no money from carrying on his crusade, but he makes plenty of enemies, many of whom own chain saws and guns. He won't back down, though, because he loves the forest and loves the creatures that depend on the forest. Hearing him talk, you realize that he sees himself as one of those creatures, like any warbler or fox.

I could multiply these examples a hundredfold without ever leaving my county. Most likely you could do the same in yours. Any community worth living in must have a web of people faithful to good work and to one another, or that community would fall apart.

To say that fidelity is common is not to say it's easy or painless or free. The man or woman who forgoes a promotion by refusing the company's offer to move across country pays a price for staying put. The parent who remains devoted to a troublesome child may come to grief. Those who are loyal to a cause or a place or an institution will almost certainly be taken advantage of by those who are loyal only to themselves. People who champion unpopular views or stand in the way of the powerful may risk more than serenity or cash; like the defender of the forest, they may even risk their necks.

Fidelity costs energy and time, maybe a lifetime. Every firm *yes* we say requires many firm *no*s. After Quaker Meeting one Sunday I was talking with the man who visited prisoners in jail, when a young woman approached, breathless with excitement, to ask if he would join the board of a new peace group she was organizing. In a rush of words she told him why the cause was crucial, why the time was ripe, why she absolutely needed his leadership. Knowing this man's sympathies, I figured he would agree to serve. But after listening to her plea, he gazed at her soberly for a moment, then said, "That is certainly a vital concern, worthy of all your passion. But it is not *my* concern." The challenge for all of us is to find those few causes which are peculiarly our own, those to which we are clearly called, and then to embrace them wholeheartedly.

If your goal is to find a center, a focus, a gathering place within your life, then you would do well to practice fidelity. By slowing down, abiding in relationships, staying in place, remaining faithful to a calling, we create the conditions for paying attention, for discovering depths, for finding a purpose and a pattern in our days. Fidelity enables us to orient ourselves, to know with some confidence where we are. It provides continuity, enabling us to see how things change, what is endangered, what persists. It keeps us from drifting, keeps us from hurrying through our days. "The reason why we don't take time is a feeling that we have to keep moving," says Thomas Merton. If we would only be still and look about, we'd realize that we already "have what we seek. We don't have to rush after it. It was there all the time, and if we give it time, it will make itself known to us."

We cannot give ourselves to every person or place, cannot answer every need, if we wish to act responsibly. Monks who follow Saint Benedict's Rule take a vow to seek spiritual transformation, as one might expect, but they also take a vow of stability, which means a commitment to the grounds of their monastery as well as to their community. The second vow is a condition for the first: outward stability provides a framework for inward change. One needn't be a monk to benefit from loyalty to a home ground. Those who stay put instead of rushing about are likelier to face the hard questions, to focus their energy on the real work. Gary Snyder offers us a secular version of this insight:

> Stewardship means, for most of us, find your place on the
> planet, dig in, and take responsibility from there—the tire-

some but tangible work of school boards, county supervisors, local foresters, local politics, even while holding in mind the largest scale of potential change. Get a sense of workable territory, learn about it, and start acting point by point.

If you imagine trying to solve all the world's problems at once, you're likely to quit before you finish rolling up your sleeves. But if you stake out your own workable territory, if you settle on a manageable number of causes, then you might accomplish a great deal, all the while trusting that others elsewhere are working faithfully in their own places.

Fidelity entails restraint. The marriage vow means choosing one lover and forsaking all others. The fact that it's broken left and right does not change the meaning of the vow. In my experience, choosing one lover and renewing that choice day by day, year by year, is not a sacrifice of freedom, the way bachelor jokes make it out to be, but a fulfillment of desire. Marriage gives meaning to desire, gives it a purpose, a history, a home. I keep faith not merely with Ruth but with myself, for the person I have become is inextricable from the life we have shared. Our travels, our meals, our walks and talks, the books we've read together, the movies and plays we've seen, the children we've brought into the world, the work we've done, our struggles and accomplishments—the sum of this mutual history defines who we are.

Having shared so much, Ruth and I sometimes communicate in lopped phrases, as though sending telegrams, a habit that irks Eva and Jesse.

"Did you—?" Ruth might say, and I might answer, "The rain—."

"Then Saturday—?"

"Charlie's teeth—."

"I see," Ruth might conclude. Whereupon one of the kids is

likely to cry, "I *don't* see. Will you two talk in complete sentences so normal people can understand!"

For a couple to be that familiar with one another's thoughts may seem stifling to young people, for whom privacy is precious, and for whom the making of a self distinct from family and friends is an urgent task. I've heard my students refer to a thoroughly wedded couple as "joined at the hip," as if the two partners had fused into a homogeneous lump. That may happen, of course, if the partners lazily surrender their separate identities, but it need not. I know many long-married folks who remain distinct individuals, as if the durability of marriage emboldens them to become ever more thoroughly themselves.

But won't marriage eventually grow stale if the partners know one another so intimately? I worried about that back when I was memorizing poems for wooing, and I suspect that Eva thinks about it now, as she prepares for her own wedding. Marriages *do* become stale if husband and wife hunker down within their old boundaries, and if either one makes the mistake of regarding the other's personality—the small ego of the self—as all there is to know. But the truth is that each person opens into depths that can never be fathomed. You will not discover those depths over a weekend or a summer, no matter how romantic, but only over the long haul, and you will never exhaust them. The more I learn of Ruth, the more she reveals to me.

In late September, barely a month after suffering heat exhaustion, I flew to Phoenix to give a speech. Before I left, Ruth said, "Now don't you go hiking in the desert and get yourself sick again." My host was going to take me backpacking in the mountains, I assured her, and in my Midwestern ignorance I envisioned cool green peaks rising above scorched flatlands.

My host and a friend of his did take me into the mountains— the enticingly named Superstition Mountains, which turned out to be neither cool nor green, but rather blistering and stony and dry, pure desert tilted uphill and down, as anyone with a rudimentary knowledge of Arizona geography would have predicted.

We parked at the trail head above Apache Lake around four in the afternoon, ate crackers smeared with avocado, shouldered our packs, and set off. Had they known the temperature, and how little water we carried, and how far we planned to hike, neither Ruth nor my doctor would have let me take a step away from the car. We didn't need to carry much water, or much food either, according to my hiking buddies, because we were headed for a green valley ten miles up in the mountains, where a stream flowed even in the driest months and where an orchard of apples would be ripe about now. A man named Reavis had planted the orchard early in this century, carried water to the young trees, protected them from varmints and thieves, and eventually began selling his crop in faraway Phoenix, hauling bags of apples on the backs of mules. Decades after Reavis died (his skull parted from the rest of his skeleton), the unpruned, unsprayed, unfertilized trees still bore generously (or so my companions had been led to believe; neither of them had made this trek before).

The biscuit-colored land, spiky with cactus and green-barked paloverde, caught at my heart, and our talk along the trail was infused with the beauty of the place. But even in this fine company, in this magnificent terrain, I kept thinking of our destination, which sounded too much like paradise to be real. Four hours into the hike, with darkness pooling in the arroyos and no hint of a green valley, we began to think we had lost the trail. As we paused to consider our fix, we caught a whiff of wood smoke, just a trace on the dry air. So we hiked on upwind, picking our way over stones in the dim light of a half moon.

Nearly an hour later we spied the gleam of a campfire and heard the murmur of voices. Avoiding these other hikers, so as not to intrude on their privacy, we made our way across a sagging fence, through implausible knee-high grass, and into the presence of trees. From their bowed and fretted shapes I could tell they were fruit trees, and from their smell I knew they were apples. The nicker of horses rose from a paddock near the campfire, and from closer by, barely audible above the sound of wind in grass, came the trickle of water. It was the sound of blessing. We would have to wait for morning light before pumping water from the creek, but tonight we could drink the last few swigs from our canteens. Before we laid out our sleeping bags under the stars, we rummaged on the ground for apples. We ate and ate until the juice ran down our chins, until the sweet flesh filled us, and then we slept.

The next day we loaded our packs with apples, a few for munching on the hike out, most for family and friends—manna from the Superstition Mountains. As I swayed along the trail that morning with this lumpy weight on my back, I couldn't decide which gave me more hope, the persistence of the trees or the persistence of the man who had tended them. Then I realized that the two forms of constancy are kin—that fidelity is a human expression of wildness. For years Reavis kept faith with his vision of an orchard in the desert, laboring to bring it about, and for even more years the apple trees have kept faith with their cycles of growth.

Back home, I presented Ruth the largest, reddest, firmest apple, to show her that I had guarded myself from heatstroke, away out there in the desert, by walking in wet and fruitful country.

It's hard to imagine Arizona heat on a winter morning in Indiana, with the windchill at twenty below. I write these lines on a January day while Ruth drives over icy roads to the town an hour away where her parents live in the Methodist Home. Her mother suffers from Alzheimer's disease, and her father has been slowed by heart attacks and strokes. Those two have suffered through alterations that no one in Shakespeare's day could have survived, and yet they remain devoted to one another and they have inspired a comparable devotion in their daughter. Over roads that a state trooper on the radio describes as "slicker than grease on glass," Ruth will carry her mother and father to doctors' appointments in Indianapolis, then to lunch, then to the drugstore and bank, then back to their apartment, where she will help them with medicine and bills, settle their worries, and rouse their spirits.

Watching Ruth care for her parents as they age, a responsibility she fulfills with good humor and grace, I consider how much harder their lives would be without her loyalty. I consider how grim the world would be for all of us without the innumerable acts of kindness and support arising from fidelity, not only of children for parents and of parents for children, not only of partners and neighbors and friends for one another, but of visionaries for their causes, workers for their jobs, citizens for their communities, inhabitants for their home ground. Such acts are so widespread, so vital to our preservation, that I cannot help thinking they arise, like wildness and healing, from our very nature. True, we must be taught the way of steadfast love, but we learn it readily.

The first Psalm of the Hebrew Bible, handed down by people who knew quite well the rigors of life in the desert, offers hope to those who obey the law of the Lord:

> They are like trees planted by streams of water,
> bearing fruit in due season, with leaves that do not wither;
> everything they do shall prosper.

Reading that now, I see an orchard hidden away in a valley of the Superstition Mountains, I hear a trickle of water through a tangle of willows, I taste the sticky apple juice on my lips. I draw courage from these tokens of fidelity, and I take delight in the Psalmist's image, even without believing that anyone knows, once and for all, the law of the Lord and without believing that good people will inevitably prosper. The universe is not set up to reward us for virtue, nor to comfort us for our losses, nor to coddle us in our pain; and yet it has, remarkably, brought us into being. How can we help wondering about the source of our existence?

Since it dawned on me at the age of ten or twelve that Creation is a great mystery, and that life and consciousness and death only compound that mystery, I have been searching for ways to understand the ultimate ground out of which all things rise. Surely this is one of the oldest human searches, older than philosophy or science, older than religion, older perhaps than speech. I have learned much from philosophy and science and from many religions, beginning with the low-temperature Christianity of my childhood, yet none of these traditions has seemed adequate to the splendor and intricacy of the world. When the apostles beg Jesus to increase their faith and Jesus answers, If you had faith even as large as a mustard seed, you could uproot trees, you could move mountains, I want to break in on that ancient conversation and cry, "Faith in *what*?" I know very well the tidy answers. But no catechism, no scriptures, no commandments, no equations seem rich or subtle enough to comprehend even a single life, let alone the universe.

Although Thomas Merton worshiped as a Trappist monk, reciting holy offices several times a day, he warned us not to be caught up in religious formulas: "The object of our faith is not a statement about God but God himself to whom the statement points and who is infinitely beyond anything the statement might lead us to imagine or understand." A Zen parable reminds us that every spiritual teaching is only a finger pointing at the moon: we must not become so obsessed by the finger that we forget the moon. The Tao that can be told is not the Tao; the Way that can be named is not the Way. Even to speak of the source and pattern of things as "God" or "Tao" is risky, since we may confuse the neat word, so easy on the tongue, with the bewildering reality.

Yet fidelity requires us to embrace *some* vision of ultimate reality—if not one of the prepackaged varieties, then one we compose ourselves. To lead a centered life, I believe, one must keep faith not only with a vocation, a mission, a person, or a place, but also with a moral ground that sanctions and upholds these loyalties. You can see the effects of such faith in any firmly grounded life.

In an earlier chapter I mentioned the example of Vaclav Havel, who said that hope is "an orientation of the spirit, an orientation of the heart; it transcends the world that is immediately experienced, and is anchored somewhere beyond its horizons." And we can look to Mohandas Gandhi, who founded his campaign of nonviolent resistance on a principle he called *satyagraha*, which means "firmly grasping the truth"; Gandhi believed that love and kindness and peace are in keeping with the nature of things, and they will therefore eventually prevail over hatred and cruelty and violence.

Neither standing by truth nor anchoring one's faith in a transcendent power guarantees that justice will vanquish injustice here and now, nor that righteousness will roll down like an ever-flowing stream, but it does give one strength to carry on. And if we receive the strength to carry on the work we believe in, with people we love, in a place we cherish, what else do we need?

NINE

SKILL

When the exaltation of wildness or family or fidelity wears off, I tumble into my body once more, down the slope of gravity and time. Where else could I dwell except in this familiar flesh, with its smooth habits and rough aches? For more than a year I've been carrying around my list of reasons for hope, and I feel the added weight of those days in my joints. I wake up rehearsing the list one Saturday morning in late summer while rain pounds the roof. My feet slide into sandals, my legs carry me to the kitchen, my hands gather makings for breakfast, all of their own accord but with abundant complaints from every last bone.

On rainy days my mother often stops by to ask about the pains in my feet, my fingers, my knees. She brings me small tins of an ointment called tiger balm, purchased in China, to rub on the sore spots. She advises me to wrap whatever hurts in heating pads, no matter how muggy the weather. She shows me how to relieve the pressure on my joints by stretching. She circles around me and frets.

Although my mother's bones began their service twenty-nine years before I was born, she's never broken any of hers, while I've snapped, dislocated, or otherwise abused quite a few of mine. As a boy I fell off bicycles and ponies, tumbled from trees, slammed into the walls of gymnasiums during basketball games, dropped toolboxes and logs on my innocent feet; as a man, I've lifted too much lumber and stone, climbed too many ladders, dug too many holes, twisted my spine too often cleaning gutters or fixing cars. My bones remember every insult. Rain sharpens their memory. I limp for an hour or so after getting out of bed each morning, and for an hour or so before going to bed each night. Following a bout of carpentry or landscaping, my stiff arms may complain about carrying a tray of dishes to the table, my hands may refuse to button a shirt.

My durable mother, meanwhile, has been waltzing and square-dancing, teaching an aerobics class at the senior center, and gardening in her backyard. Still without any broken bones, she only began to slow down a few years ago when arthritis flamed in her left knee. The summer before Jesse and I went tramping in the Rockies, the pain in her knee grew so bad that she ground nearly to a halt. For months she debated whether to have the joint replaced. At her age (well past seventy) would she ever heal? In the end she had to choose between risking the operation or camping forever in an easy chair with her feet propped up, and she chose the operation. She spent three days in a clinic, six weeks in a convalescent home, and six months in physical therapy, wondering all the while if she would ever be able to dance or garden or teach aerobics again.

A hard year passed. Performing exercises to limber up the scarred knee, riding a stationary bicycle to strengthen the withered leg, she winced, she wept, but she persevered. I ached in sympathy, wishing I could do some of the agonizing work for her. I offered her tiger balm. Eventually she regained her old ease of motion, thanks to her determined efforts, and thanks also to the therapists who nursed her along, the surgeon who performed the operation, the people who fashioned the artificial joint, those who manufactured the materials from which the joint was made, and the countless souls through the ages who've discovered and perfected the many ways of medicine. By the time Jesse and I hiked up into the Wild Basin, she was back in full swing.

Now, two years after the operation, she walks without a hitch, leads exercise classes, spins around ballrooms to the music of big bands, raises gladioli and raspberries and rhubarb to give away. I'm happy for my mother, and also happy for my species, that we have figured out how to achieve such healing. Her knee bends sweetly again because of human skill wedded to the body's wild powers of recovery. In this alliance of wildness and craft I find another item for my medicine bundle, another source of hope. I wish to speak here about our capacity for making and mending things; I wish to celebrate not only the good that we accomplish but the gifts of meaning and delight that we receive from doing skillful work.

Before the celebration, though, a caution: if we practice our skills without foresight or compassion, we're headed for trouble—as individuals and as a species. No sooner do we learn how to smelt iron than we begin forging swords. We capture the explosion of gasoline in cylinders to drive horseless buggies and before long we're smothering the earth with pavement and filling the air with smog. We split the atom and build a bomb. Every time we unriddle another disease, we burden the planet with more hungry mouths to feed and more itchy minds to satisfy. Now we're monkeying with genes, and who knows what troublesome creatures we may loose upon the scene? Many of the nightmares about the future that ruin the sleep of my students and my children could be traced back to our blundering cleverness in manipulating the world.

Once young people begin to notice how often we misuse our ingenuity—to increase the levels of nicotine in cigarettes, to make handguns more lethal, to poison wolves, to fill our airwaves with trash—they may grow discouraged by our potential for mischief. I certainly felt discouraged when I was Jesse's age, or Eva's. After a childhood infatuation with science, when I believed that whatever we figured out how to do we should blithely do, I came to feel that the earth would be far better off if we forgot every trick we knew. It seemed to me, in my late teens and early twenties, during my years of dawning political and ecological awareness provoked by the Vietnam War, that our whole civilization, the sum of all those skills laboriously acquired and passed on through the ages, had culminated in napalm, B-52s, electronic bingo, flip-top beer cans, water skis, alligator-skin shoes, and soap operas. Other species would heave a sigh of relief, I figured, if we all retreated to our rooms and sat very still and did nothing for a long while.

I've never been any good at doing nothing, however. So I finished college, married Ruth, went off to graduate school in England, where I read mind-changing books, agitated against the war, marched in support of sundry causes, scoured a good many spiritual traditions for guidance, then came back to start a job in America, where I began teaching young people who were as eager and baffled as I had ever been, and by and by I helped give birth to a child. More than anything else, Eva's arrival hauled me out of my funk. How could I gaze into those brand-new eyes in the delivery room of a hospital, surrounded by deft people and cunning machines, and think that all our ingenuity is for naught? How could I dismiss as evil all those inventions that would ease my daughter's way through life?

Of course, our power to manipulate the world is neither wholly benign, as I thought in my childhood, nor wholly destructive, as I thought for a spell in early adulthood, but rather, like most human powers, a mixed blessing. The same day I wrote in praise of the surgeon who repaired my mother's knee, I read in the newspaper about a plastic surgeon who specializes in disguising the faces of criminals. The two doctors may be equally adroit with a scalpel, but one cures the lame while the other hides crooks. Everything depends on how we use our skills. Thieves and assassins may be good at what they do, yet what they do is nonetheless evil. Masons and carpenters may build houses or gas chambers with the same tools; pilots may deliver mail or missiles; engineers may design space telescopes or styrofoam burger boxes; chemists may purify aspirin or heroin; writers may compose sober histories or tabloid sleaze.

It's easy to praise the surgeon who repaired my mother's knee, or the astronomers who track comets, or the ecologists who restore damaged habitats; it's easy to honor the desert apple grower who watered and pruned his orchards in the Superstition Mountains, or the South African trumpeter who filled street urchins with the juice of jazz. But what about artists who design the billboards that blight our highways? What about loggers who cut down the last of the old-growth forests? What about assembly line workers who build gas-guzzling cars? What about computer hackers who meddle in other people's lives? What about lawyers who chase ambulances or hunters who chase elephants? What about generals, gamblers, developers, lobbyists, fashion designers, talk-show hosts, or exotic dancers? They may be wizards at their work, dazzling to watch. Yet on balance do they add to or subtract from the good of the world? That's a hard question to answer, but it's the crucial one to ask. In order to judge any exercise of skill, we should ask not only what it does for the person, what rewards of money or pleasure it brings; we should also ask what it does for other people, how well it serves their needs and how genuine those needs are; and we should ask what effect it has on other creatures and on the earth.

I have a friend who plays the violin exquisitely, with a grace that makes audiences weep, and I have another friend who plays the stock market shrewdly, buying and selling hundreds of shares every hour. The violinist brings fresh beauty into the world, at very little cost to anyone except herself, for those thousands of hours of practice. The stock speculator adds nothing to the world's wealth, but merely transfers money from the hands of more patient investors into his own. I rejoice at how the violinist uses her skill and regret how the speculator uses his.

Similarly, one can admire the talent on display in a television ad and still lament that so much expertise is devoted to peddling casinos or colas. One can respect the skill required to negotiate a hostile takeover of one corporation by another, while concluding that the effects of the takeover may be harmful to everyone except the shareholders. One can acknowledge the skill required to knock a small white ball across a carpet of grass into a hole, or to hit a somewhat larger ball over a fence, or to dunk an even larger ball backwards through a steel hoop, while still recognizing that we as a nation waste fantastic amounts of money and time worshiping those who are expert at basketball or baseball or golf.

Just as one sign of maturity is the willingness to accept limits, and thereby to live in fidelity, so another is the willingness to make judgments of value. The word *skill* rises from a root meaning to cut apart or separate, signifying the power of discernment. The seasoned carpenter knows not only how to use tools well, but which hammer or saw to choose for a given task, which board, which nails or screws, and knows also how to assess the results. One day while I carried two-by-fours to a builder who was framing a new house, he told me he wouldn't let his worst dog sleep in a house put up by a rival contractor, a man known for cheap and shoddy work. "He ought to go apologize to the trees," the builder said, "for the way he mistreats wood." If we cared less about how much money or fame people earn by practicing their skills and cared more about how much good or harm they do, we would all be better off. The ability to judge with clear eyes how skills are used—whether to enrich or diminish life, whether to improve our days or squander them—is itself a prime example of skill.

Blessed with a new knee, Mother only winces and staggers for balance nowadays when going up or down stairs. Her own house, one story high and built on a slab, poses no challenge; but our two-story house, with a threshold some eight or ten feet above the level of the street, confronts her with steps inside and out.

The stairways inside have banisters, but until recently those between house and street had none. If anybody was home when Mother arrived, one of us would go outside to offer her an arm as she climbed up from the sidewalk. But when nobody was home, she had to labor up and down on her own.

The danger of her falling convinced Ruth and me that we must have some railings, one for the steps near the street, one for the steps at the front door. I thought of making them from wood, but worried about splinters. The one-size-fits-all railing kits for sale at the lumber yard were too flimsy. The only option left was to have them custom-made from steel. So I asked around for a good welder and was given the name of Earl Ketchum, on Mt. Gilead Road. When I showed up with my sketch, Earl was kneeling on the floor of his shop, surrounded by hoses, gauges, tanks filled with explosive gases, and by enough rods and tubes and steel plates to build a ship. A rangy man of about forty, with hands as broad as platters, he was laying out the pieces for a trailer hitch, following a design marked in pencil on the concrete. The ghostly patterns of earlier jobs, partly erased, covered the floor like faded tattoos. What I could see of Earl's own skin was pockmarked by dozens of burns, especially at the base of his throat, where the welding mask would not reach, and along his forearms, where drops of molten metal would sometimes cut through even the heaviest leather gloves.

I handed Earl my sketch and asked if he'd give me an estimate for a pair of railings.

He pinched my careful drawing between scorched thumb and index finger, eyed it skeptically, muttered, "I might," then handed me the paper and resumed work on the trailer hitch.

I stood there waiting for some further word. None came, so I asked, "Would you like my name and address and phone number?"

"It wouldn't hurt."

I tore a page from my notebook, scribbled the information, offered it to Earl.

"Just lay it on the bench," he said, waving at a battered steel table. I could have parked my car on its top, the bench was so big, except that every square foot of the surface was already heaped with blueprints and tools and parts. I cleared a corner and left my note there, pinned under a tape measure.

"So you'll come by sometime and give me an estimate?" I suggested.

Earl grunted but never looked up from his trailer hitch.

As I backed out of the shop, figuring I wouldn't lay eyes on Earl again, I thought to add, "My mother's been having trouble getting up and down those steps ever since she had a knee joint replaced, and I worry she might fall without anything to hang on to."

Now Earl peered up at me, with eyes squinted from staring through smoked glass at bright flames. "She live with you?"

"No, but she lives in town, and she visits us."

He loosed a huff of breath. "Well, then. Guess I'd better make her some railings. Where'd you leave your name?"

I pointed at the note and this time he looked, saying, "All right, then. I'll come by when I get a chance."

Earl did come by a few weeks later, a towering man now that I saw him upright, half a foot higher than my own six feet, wide enough to fill a doorway, the whole expanse wrapped in coveralls the shade of butterscotch. Faded blue denim showed through holes at the knees and elbows like pale patches of sky. As he sized up the job he told me about his youngest boy's weekend feats in football. "He just flattens everybody on his way to the end zone," Earl said. A heavy cold made his big voice sound as though it was booming from inside a closet.

"Is he taking after you?" I asked.

"Like a bear after honey," said Earl.

Using level and tape, he measured the steps, then recorded the figures on a scrap of cardboard with a pencil retrieved from behind his ear. After a minute's calculation, he gave me an estimate for the cost of two railings. The figure seemed fair to me, so we shook hands, and his great paw swallowed mine. "No telling when I'll get to it," he said, "I'm so buried in work."

"I sure would like to have those railings in place before the first snow."

"Oh, I'll aim to beat the snow. We don't want your mom slipping and sliding."

Earl paused to study the sidewalk, which a crew from the city had replaced a few weeks earlier. He laid his level on the new concrete to make sure water would drain away from the base of the steps. Then he paced the length of the walk, checking the joints and the textured finish. At the end of his inspection, he announced, "The boys did a good job."

"I thought so," I said.

"You thought right." He climbed in his truck and hooked an arm through the window. "You want anything fancy on those railings? Any curlicues or doodads?"

"Just make them simple and strong," I answered.

"Black or white?"

"Black."

"You got it," said Earl, and away he drove.

Of all the exhibits I studied in the British Museum, the one I found the most moving, even more so than the Assyrian lions or the figurines of women holding out their breasts, was a case filled with stoneworking tools from Egypt. Among the items, all dating from the second millennium B.C.E., there were dividers for measuring, a stylus for marking, chisels pitted with rust, a try square, and a wooden mallet, its angled face gouged from delivering hundreds of thousands of blows. I thought of the long-dead hands that once wielded those tools and the eyes that guided them, thought of how those hands and eyes had carved statues, raised monuments, inscribed hieroglyphics, fit block to block in pyramids and palaces. I was moved by a feeling of kinship with those vanished craftsmen, for I have my own banged-

up mallets and chisels, and by a realization that virtually everything they knew about their craft had been passed down from
master to apprentice, from their time to ours, over three thousand years.

There are men and women in my part of Indiana today who
carve limestone using techniques that would have been familiar
to those ancient Egyptians. I've spent hours in the quarries and
mills watching them work. They use air-powered hammers these
days instead of wooden mallets, and their chisels are made of
harder metals, but the square and stylus and dividers haven't
changed shape, and the carving of stone is still the same old col-
laboration of hand and eye. These skills have been preserved for
the best of reasons—because they're useful, because they're sat-
isfying, and because elders have taken pains to teach them to
the young.

The knack of shaping stone can be traced back far earlier than
the second millennium B.C.E., of course, back through petro-
glyphs and megaliths, flint scrapers and hand axes, back to the
very emergence of our kind from the company of apes. When I
was a boy in Ohio I walked the freshly plowed fields each spring,
on the lookout for arrowheads. Most years I found one, sometimes two or three, and every time I marveled at how anything so
lethal could be so beautiful. I scrubbed the points clean with
spit and rubbed them dry on my jeans and immediately the scal-
loped wedges of stone gleamed as though lit from within. I
wrapped them in cotton and kept them in the drawer with my
socks. Now and again I would take one out, run my fingers gingerly over the sharp edges, and try to imagine how it had been
made, how it had been lost, and whether it had ever been used to
kill anything.

By the time I moved from those Ohio fields, I'd given away
most of my arrowheads to bosom buddies or curious visitors, but
I kept a few prize ones. I keep them still, in a wooden cigar box on
a shelf beside my writing desk. Between sentences I often pick

one up, turn it over and over, still marveling. I now realize these arrowheads were shaped only a few centuries ago, by the Shawnee or Miami or other woodland tribes. Yet to me as a boy they seemed to have been handed down from the dawn of time. And in a sense they were, for these stone points embody skills that were already developing in the valleys of Africa more than two million years ago.

I mean *embody* as more than a metaphor. The design of tools and the knowledge of how to use them flow from body to body, mind to mind, through the millennia, each generation adding its own discoveries. If the elders are diligent in training the young and if the young are eager to learn, skills accumulate over time, so that today's engineers or gymnasts or surgeons may outdo even the greatest of their predecessors. We're no smarter than our ancestors, no more talented, yet we benefit from all their efforts, just as those who come after us will benefit from ours.

If the flow of knowledge is interrupted, however, skills may be lost. I know perhaps half as much as my father did about woodworking, because in my adult years, living far from him, I could only go for lessons once or twice a year, and he died before I could complete my schooling. Antonio Stradivari carried the secrets of his violin-making with him to the grave. While we can learn a great deal by studying the violins themselves, we cannot learn everything, for certain critical steps were known to Stradivari alone. On several occasions in the past, brilliant mathematicians, in writing down proofs of some new insight, have truncated their argument—saying, in effect, the rest is obvious—and no subsequent mathematician has been able to fill in the gaps. Every time the last native speaker of a language falls silent, as bullets and disease and global culture wipe out indigenous peoples around the world, we lose one more distinctive way of seeing, one more set of insights about living in a place.

Even when knowledge is more widely held, it still depends for survival on faithful teachers and willing pupils. There are farm-

ers scattered across the United States who know how to plow
with horses rather than tractors, how to raise livestock and crops
without depleting the soil, how to increase the land's fertility and
the abundance of wildlife. But their numbers are dwindling,
while a new generation of farmers learns only the quick-and-
dirty industrial scheme that relies on pesticides, herbicides, artificial fertilizers, and an endless supply of petroleum and topsoil.
A time may come when the last of those who know the wise old
ways die out. If that happens, and we discover we need those lost
skills, we'll have to relearn them from scratch, aided by hints
from books, films, or photographs, but relying mainly on the slow
stumble of trial and error, the tedium of practice and more
practice.

We'd be far better off conserving the old skills instead of having to resurrect them; yet the fact remains that we can, to a remarkable degree, resurrect them. From studying the debris at
tool-making sites around the world, for example, anthropologists
have recovered many of the techniques for shaping stone points.
They can't be sure their methods are exactly the same as the ancient ones, of course, but the results are of comparable quality. I
have watched a latter-day expert cleave a lump of flint with the
sharp blow of a stone hammer on a bone punch, then cleave it
again to produce a flake of suitable size, and then fashion a
deadly and beautiful arrowhead by chipping the edges with the
tip of an antler, all with amazing precision and speed, as though
he'd apprenticed himself to the ancients themselves and not
merely to their artifacts.

There's not much call for arrowheads these days, except as objects of study or admiration. Pottery, on the other hand, is still as
useful today as it was in the time of King Ashurbanipal, whose
craftsmen carved those bas-reliefs of leaping lions twenty-six
hundred years ago, or in the time of our ancestors who figured
out how to fire clay into ceramics some ten thousand years ago.
The people of Acoma, a Hopi pueblo in New Mexico, have been

making pottery for many centuries, going on foot to the same quarry for clay, using the same minerals from the desert for coloring glazes. Yet certain traditional designs were lost when European invasions disrupted the passing on of knowledge to the young. Left with nothing but shards of the antique pots, including sacred vessels used in burials, the Hopi lost track of the old designs for a time, and have been able to recover them only in recent decades.

A potter from Acoma laughed when she told me how the recovery had come about: "My mother went to the museum and looked at pots the scientists had glued back together. She drew pictures, right there in front of the glass cases, and she brought the pictures home." As the woman spoke she was grinding minerals in a mortar. Now she paused to rub a pinch of the dust between index finger and thumb, judging the texture. When she resumed grinding, she resumed talking. "We looked everywhere on our own land, but only found what we needed in the museum. Think of the poor scientists digging in the hot sun and picking up tiny pieces! So much work!" Again the potter laughed. "First, the white grandfathers tried to break us apart and now their grandsons try to put us back together."

Grandsons and granddaughters alike, light-skinned or dark, can in fact repair much of the damage wrought by previous generations. It may be more difficult to mend broken communities and habitats than to mend pots, but it is still possible. We have that power; we have that opportunity. To use it, we'll need to preserve the legacy of skills that enhance life—everything from articulate speech to antiseptic surgery, from pottery to carpentry, from breeding plants and baking bread to measuring gravity and mapping the stars. We'll need to relearn some vital skills that enabled our ancestors to live well at less cost to the earth, such as those required for raising and cooking more of our own food, for building modest shelters out of local materials, for stitching our clothes and fixing our machines, for entertaining ourselves and our neighbors. And we'll need to develop new skills for new conditions, as restoration ecologists and computer modelers and international peacekeepers are now doing. If we learn a useful craft and practice it well, if we serve the real needs of other people and other creatures, then we'll not only tap the springs of satisfaction for ourselves, we'll also help in the labor of healing.

A month after taking his measurements and well before the first snow, Earl Ketchum showed up at our place with a handsome pair of railings, free of doodads or curlicues, each with banisters and posts fashioned from square tubing, balusters spaced every four inches, all the joints neatly welded without so much as a ripple in the beads of steel, the whole affair painted matte black and sturdy enough to stop a truck. Out of his own dented pickup, Earl unloaded a toolbox, a framing square, a level half as long as he was, a dustpan and broom, a drill the size of a jackhammer, and a slurry of mortar in a bucket.

He propped one of the railings on the steps leading down to the sidewalk and squinted at me. "Look okay?"

"It looks just fine," I answered.

"I'd say so."

He marked where the holes should go, then tapped a steel punch into each mark to make sure the point of the drill bit stayed where it should. "You plug me in?" he asked.

I dragged a thick power cord up the sidewalk and plugged it into an outlet on the front porch, then gave Earl a thumbs-up. He steadied the bit against the instep of his boot, gripped the drill by its pair of jutting handles, and squeezed the switch. Soon a gray spiral of powdered concrete rose up the winding shaft of the bit. Every now and again Earl would blow the hole clean of dust and check it for depth; he did this more and more often as he neared his goal, until finally he was satisfied. Once the holes were drilled, he lowered the railing into place, measured and leveled and squared it from every direction, then poured the slurry of mortar around each post, tamping the soupy mixture with a dowel to squeeze out any pockets of air. Finally he braced the railing with scraps of angle iron, so that it would stay square and true while the concrete hardened.

"You figure that'll keep your mom on her pins?" he asked.

"It ought to," I answered.

Earl backed off and circled around to give the railing the stern test of his experienced eye. Noticing a flaw in the paint, he fetched a spray can from the truck and covered the blemish with a fresh black coat. "You touch it up every spring and it'll never rust," he said. "Why, my dad put in that railing for the Alamedas, down there on the corner"—he pointed toward the end of our block—"back around 1955 or '57, and they keep it painted, and you can see it's as good as new."

"Your father was a welder?"

He was, Earl told me, and so was his grandfather. Earl had tagged along after them from the time he could walk, and he never wanted to be anything else but a welder. He helped his father put up railings all over the place, fix tractors, patch up derricks and saws in the limestone mills, fabricate just about anything you could make out of steel. His dad was retired now, crippled with arthritis, but sometimes on a Sunday he and Earl would drive around town to see how their work was holding up. Earl had welded everything from bicycle frames to coolant pipes for nuclear reactors. Now he was teaching the trade to his son, the one who flattens everybody on his way to the end zone.

"My only worry about that boy," said Earl, "is that he'll be so good at football he won't want to mess with welding."

"You really think he might?"

By now Earl had installed the second railing and had put away his tools, and he was sweeping powdered concrete into the dustpan. He paused to consider my question, leaning on the handle of his broom. "Naw," he said finally, "he'll be a welder. It's in him too deep."

I thanked Earl, paid him, and shook his giant hand. Before pulling away in the dented truck, he said, "Remember, keep it painted."

By the time the rain stops this sultry morning, my bones have quit aching. I hear a car door slam, and look out from my second floor window to see Mother climbing the lower steps from the street, her nimbus of white hair bobbing, one hand braced on the railing, the other wrapped around a bouquet of lavender gladioli. I go down to meet her, but she beats me to the front door, where she holds onto the porch railing while offering me the flowers. They're gorgeous. I promise to put them in a vase right away and ask if she can stay for lemonade. No, she has too many errands to run—clothes to sort at Hospitality House, a bright-eyed girl to tutor at the middle school, more bouquets to deliver.

"But first," she says, "how's your knee? I worry about you whenever it rains."

"It's fine," I tell her. "How's yours?"

"Oh, I hardly ever think about it. I don't pick up heavy weights and I'm careful about my turns when I'm dancing." Holding the railing, she gives a playful curtsy, knees bent outward, like a ballerina at the bar. "Well, have to run!" And once down the porch stairs she nearly does run, hurrying off without a limp. She slows up at the steps near the street, grabs the railing carefully, eases her way down, then bustles to her car. Before zooming away, she waves at me and calls back cheerfully, "That welder certainly did a good job. I'm thankful every time I come by."

I put the gladioli in a vase and drop an aspirin in the water to make them last. Each of the long curving stems tapers from tight green buds at the top to fully opened blooms at the bottom. I stare into one of the lavender blossoms, past the gathering of petals like crushed silk, past the curving stamens, down into the pale throat dusted with pollen, and for a moment I envy the bees.

·   ·   ·

Earl the welder is teaching his son a craft that has been handed
on, with an expanding repertoire of techniques, since the Bronze
Age. Every skill we depend on today can be traced back through
such a human lineage, sometimes shorter, sometimes longer. A
legacy of skills acquired over a few thousand or even a few hundred thousand years may seem modest compared to that inherited by most other species. The screech owl roosting in the hemlock tree beside my house employs hunting methods that have
been evolving for perhaps sixty million years. The hemlock itself,
bearing seeds in cones, performs a trick that is nearly a quarter of
a billion years old.

By comparison with these veterans, we humans are raw begin-
ners. But we learn fast, and part of what we've learned is how to
store and pass on our knowledge outside of our genes, in language and pictures, in rituals and lessons, in gesture and voice.
Do you wish to weave the seat of a chair out of split oak? Solve a
differential equation? Make a dovetail joint? Conjugate a verb?
Bake a cherry pie? Clean up a watershed or mend an arthritic
knee? Anybody alive today can find out how to do almost anything that humans have ever done, if not from the experts themselves then from the records they have left.

This rapid, cumulative learning can be a danger as well as a
blessing, as I've said. Without ignoring the danger, I find hope in
the accumulation of skill. I'm not encouraged by the mere piling
up of wealth, the proliferation of gadgets and machines, or the
tightening of our grip on nature, all those trends that form the
usual notion of progress; but I am deeply encouraged by the
steady refinement of our abilities, as individuals and as a species,
to work intelligently with the materials of earth, to collaborate
with wildness. We carry in our minds, we hold in our hands, the
power to bring about a more elegant, peaceful, and becoming existence for all creatures.

TEN

MOUNTAIN
MUSIC III

CARRYING ONLY WAIST PACKS and water bottles and snow-shoes, Jesse and I set out from our campsite along North St. Vrain Creek and headed for Thunder Lake, a thousand feet higher and four miles farther on. We soon climbed beyond the last patches of bare ground, then paused to strap on our snow-shoes. This was the moment Jesse had been waiting for since reaching the Rockies, the moment that would separate him from the casual day-trippers and prove that he was really in the wilds. With a whoop he dashed on up the trail, powder flying.

I followed slowly, knowing my limitations, and also wishing to savor the land, to notice details, to saunter instead of rushing through. In spite of my deliberate pace, I didn't resent Jesse's hurrying. When I was his age, without the means of traveling far from my Ohio home, I used to run barefoot in our woods until my feet bled; I shinnied up the tallest trees while limbs bent under me; I rode ornery ponies until they bucked me off, then scrambled back into the saddle; I worked in sweltering weather de-tasseling corn or baling hay, and in cold weather gathering maple sap, less for the money than for the satisfaction of knowing I could hold up through all that labor. Even though I no longer had the stamina to keep pace with him, I understood Jesse's craving to measure himself against river, rockface, mountain slope.

Most young men yearn for a test of their strength. Feeling their own juices flowing, they wish to confront what is most wild and rugged in the land. In durable cultures, grown men teach the young ones how to carry out these trials of endurance, how to flex their muscular will without hurting themselves or tearing up the community. This task is easier where there is an abundance of open land and a call for hard physical work. A man who spends his days hunting or farming, building houses or clearing roads, learns what his strength can do and where his limits are. In the wilds, sooner or later, even the brashest man comes up against a power greater than himself. In our society, as wild lands dwindle and jobs demanding strength and courage disappear, many young men end up testing themselves on the street. The proliferation of gangs and drugs, the shootings and car wrecks, the swelling prison population, the waywardness of so many soldiers and athletes, all suggest that we often fail in teaching our sons how to harness their fearful energy.

Jesse waited for me at a bend in the trail that gave a view to the west, where Ogalalla Peak, Isolation Peak, and Mount Alice marked the Continental Divide. Billowy clouds were gathering above the ridge, casting shadows on the steep white flanks.

"I don't like the looks of that sky," Jesse said.

"Maybe it'll blow on past," I suggested.

"Maybe." He gave me an assessing look, from snowshoes to floppy hat. "You doing okay?"

"Just fine," I answered. And it was true, even though the going was tough, not merely uphill, zigzagging along switchbacks, but also up and down over windcarved drifts and over the slippery backs of boulders. The morning's unexpected freshness and clarity had stayed with me. The longer our truce held, the lighter I felt.

As we continued on, Jesse still made lunging dashes on ahead, but he circled back more often, maybe to check on me, maybe to see what I thought of the darkening sky. I thought less and less well of it as we climbed. The flat bottoms of the clouds blurred with rain, and they were sliding our way. Rain at this altitude would chill us badly and make the footing treacherous. With such a depth of snow, avalanches were always a possibility. But the greatest danger was from lightning. Although still a thousand feet below tree line, the fir and spruce were thinning out, so we hiked more and more in the open, making handy targets for any loose electricity.

One of the times he circled back to join me, Jesse asked, "Did you hear thunder?"

"We're aiming for Thunder Lake, aren't we?"

"Seriously, Dad."

I stood still and listened, but could hear only wind through needled branches. "Nothing yet."

"Do you want to keep going?"

I looked at this boy who kept astonishing me by having grown into a man, now an inch taller than I, with a ginger beard on his jaw and thick arms crossed over his chest. Yet the child was not so far below the surface, for the skin of his face had only just begun to show the marks of sun and grief.

"Do you?"

He gazed up the trail. "We must be getting close."

"Under a mile, I'd guess."

"Let's try it," he said, shuffling on over the snow.

Halfway up another switchback, where the few scrubby trees reached only waist high, we both stopped abruptly, as if we had run into a great hand. Now the rumble was unmistakable. We looked at one another, then at the mountains looming dark ahead. Lightning cracked the gloom, once, twice, again, again, and each bolt sent a shudder through the air. A year earlier I would have played the father, announcing that it was high time for turning around. But now I wanted Jesse to make the decision. He stood with hands on hips, quite still, watching the storm. Between rolls of thunder I could hear him panting. I waited, my own fear rising.

At length he said, "Rain I could take, but I don't want to mess with lightning."

I nodded but still did not speak. The air shook.

After another minute, he said quietly, "I think we'd better go back."

"You're sure?"

"I'm sure."

"Then you lead." I stepped aside to let him pass.

We started downhill at a sober pace, resisting panic, but as the sky boomed behind us and our legs caught the knack of sliding on the snowshoes, we sped up. Soon we were leaping over drifts that we had struggled to climb, skidding through swales, now and again tumbling, dusting ourselves off, and charging on. Somewhere in our breakneck descent, as I watched Jesse romp on down through avenues of pines and heard his jubilant shouts, I realized that his fear had given way to exhilaration, and so had mine.

The storm rumbled on past without dropping any rain on our camp. The snow had soaked our boots, though, so we propped them on a log with their tongues hanging out, as though they were gulping air. Late afternoon sun slipped beneath the clouds and poured light down the hillside, picking out lichen-spangled granite, the ruddy trunks of lodgepole pines, and hummocks of snow. Here the drifts were only a couple of feet deep, their white surfaces littered with needles and twigs and cones, tapering away to nothing at the edge. Water trickled from those edges, glistened on the ground, and ran toward the booming creek.

Still warm from our downhill dash, I filled cooking pots in the creek, then lugged the water back uphill and chose a boulder in full sunlight as the spot for a bath. The water was only a few degrees above freezing, so I clenched my teeth before pouring the first scoop over my head. For a few seconds my body could not decide whether to shout pain or pleasure, and then, as the salt and dirt washed away and the sun hit my skin, it settled on pleasure. While I lathered, a hummingbird cruised up, hovered a few seconds with needle beak pointing at my belly, as though deciding whether I was a rival for his territory, then zipped off. He returned for another inspection while I rinsed, hovering long enough to show me the red throat and green crown that marked him as a male broad-tailed hummer. "Relax, I'm only passing through," I said, and away he zoomed. My laugh was loud enough for Jesse to hear me up by the tent.

"What's so funny?" he called.

"A hummingbird," I called back.

"Sounds hilarious."

"You had to be there."

"I guess so."

It was sheer delight to stand there tingling from the scrubbing and the cold, and to feel the muted sun on my skin. My body was bearing up well so far, even the long-suffering joints of knee and foot and the cranky muscles of my back. I would turn fifty in a few months, yet I was far from old. Wasn't I far from old? My legs bending to slide into dry jeans, arms flexing to pull a clean shirt over my head, chest filling with sweet air, every part of me seemed brand-new. At this rate I'd be able to go tramping with Jesse for years and years.

When I got back to my notebook, I would add "Body Bright" to my list of reasons for hope.

Feeling cocky, I lifted a foot to put on a sock, and there, under the pale skin between ankle and heel, were the blue veins of my father's foot. I remembered wondering as a boy why my father had those rivery lines where my own skin was clear. Noticing them again in his last years, when the tiny vessels had begun to fray, I had realized that his body was breaking down. Now, after a day of hiking with my own grown son, gazing at my battered foot, I became at once child and adult, full of youth and full of days.

I found Jesse reading on his bench while a red squirrel chattered down at him from a nearby limb.

"Well, that makes one of us who's clean," I said.

Without lowering his book, he answered, "My mom taught me never to bathe in ice water."

"Your mom may be right," I said, chilled now that I was out of the sun. Thinking of Ruth, and of the way her face would shine when she saw us coming in the door, I realized how eager I was to tell her about our trip. It was an eagerness I felt whenever I traveled, a longing that embraced not only Ruth but also the house we shared, our children and parents, our neighbors and friends, and the Indiana countryside.

Searching for a word that would remind me of the joy and courage I drew from thoughts of home, I settled on "Fidelity."

The gray jays fluttered up, settled on a branch almost within reach, and resumed their jabbering. The red squirrel, as though relieved at shift change, moved on.

"Sounds like the bosses are back," said Jesse, closing his book. "Must be supper time. I'll cook if you wash."

"It's a deal."

As the water boiled for our fettuccine, I walked to a clearing where I could check the sky. It was a startling blue, mottled with a few cumulus clouds that were drifting slowly eastward, their backsides lit by the setting sun. Mountain chickadees crisscrossed in the air. Far above them a jet liner cruised from east to west, so high that the wings were barely visible and the fuselage gleamed like a silver needle. I had ridden up there often; Jesse and I had flown to Colorado, and would be flying home at the end of the week. Even while I regretted the burning of oil and fouling of air, and felt guilty every time I boarded a plane, I was forced to admire the audacity and ingenuity that made such travel possible. A species that can figure out how to launch a village's worth of people high in the air and hurtle them along at hundreds of miles per hour and bring them safely down again should be able to figure out how to survive without devouring the earth. Our cleverness had brought on most of our troubles, from overpopulation to nuclear waste. There was surely no way out of those troubles, without harnessing and redirecting that very cleverness. To my list of reasons for hope, I added "Skill."

I returned to the aromatic neighborhood of the stove, where Jesse was stirring the noodles.

"What did you see?" he asked.

"An airplane."

"Amazing. First a hummingbird, then an airplane. Was that your first one?"

"No, I was at Kitty Hawk when the Wright Brothers launched theirs."

"Back around the time you invented the wheel?"

"Right around then."

Jesse laughed, then filled our plates with food.

I could have put no price on that laughter, nor on the day of peace leading up to it. Freed from calendars and clocks, away from cars and money and television, here in the mountains where Jesse needed no permission from me and I required no obedience from him, we could simply be companions. Here, neither of us was in charge. There was nothing here to remind me of the world's sickness, nothing to provoke in me the anger and grief that had cast a shadow over Jesse's vision. That might well change, I realized, as soon as we drove back to Denver, put up at a motel, returned the rental car, hurried to catch a plane. But for now the truce held. When it broke down, in the days or months ahead, we would still have this place, this time, as a measure of what is durable and desirable.

After supper I went to sit on a jutting granite ledge overlooking the creek. The water crashed and roiled through a jumble of boulders, churning up an icy mist and turning the current even whiter than the surrounding snow. I pulled up the hood of my jacket, stuffed hands into pockets, and hunkered down to soak in the spray and roar.

Before long Jesse came to join me, bringing his sleepmat to sit on, and mine as well.

I thanked him, sliding the mat between me and the chilly granite.

"No problem," he said, and settled in to read.

Glacial air poured down the creek from snowfields higher up. The branches of spruce and fir, spreading outward from the banks, framed the white cascade in green lace. The day was catching up with me, and I could feel weariness gathering in my bones. I drew my knees up and wrapped my arms around them for warmth. Still I trembled. I couldn't tell whether my shivering was from the cold or from the spell of moving water.

As I hunched forward I noticed a brownish cord of some sort cupped in a hollow of the granite near my feet, among lichens and mosses and grit. Leaning closer, I could see that it was a necklace, quite slender, made of shell and stone. I first thought to leave it there, in case the person who lost it came looking, but then I realized that it must have been lying in the cavity for some time, because the moss had partly covered it. So I drew it out, brushed off the grit, and showed it to Jesse.

"Neat," he said, absently touching his own necklace of beads and braided string, one of several he had made.

"Do you want it?" I asked.

"No, that one came to you. Try it on."

I have never worn necklaces, or any other jewelry aside from my wedding ring. But I followed Jesse's advice and tried this one on, and it felt cool and smooth against my neck.

"It looks good," he said. "Dad the hippie."

He went back to reading, tilting his book to catch what little daylight there was, turning the pages with gloved hands. Eventually he gave up, closed the book, and flopped on his belly to watch the creek.

"Do you want to try Thunder Lake again tomorrow?" I asked.

"No. We've already seen most of that trail. I'd rather go up to Bluebird Lake. It's higher and the snow up there should be deeper."

"Sounds fine to me."

The water poured on. We breathed mist.

After a while, Jesse murmured, "This is a good place."

"It is."

"Thanks for bringing me here."

"I wouldn't have come without you."

In the waning light, the trees along the banks merged into a velvety blackness, and the froth of the creek shone like the Milky Way. Waves rose from the current, temporary shapes that would eventually dissolve, like my father's body or like mine, like the mountains, like the earth and stars. I blinked at my son, who rode the same current and who only asked to live out his days with a sense of hope. I would do everything in my power to help him accomplish that, beginning with an effort to climb out of the shadows and to see differently. I would never be able to look at a strip mine or a strip mall, at acres of blacktop or miles of trash, and see them as beautiful, see them as a fulfillment of earth's promise, but I could learn to see *through* them to the great renewing springs in body and land, in love and community, in human skill and stories and art.

I touched my throat as Jesse had touched his. "Mom will see this necklace and figure pretty soon I'll take up drumming."

"She'll think it's cool," he replied.

Again I imagined telling Ruth about the trip. She would hear about the furious yelling in Big Thompson Canyon, and the rafting in Poudre Canyon. She would hear about the elk chasing the coyote, the owls calling, Jupiter and Mars chasing the moon. She would hear how I stood naked in sunshine on a boulder surrounded by hummocks of snow, drenched in bliss. She would hear about the lightning that turned us back from Thunder Lake, the hummingbird that looked me over, the necklace hidden in a mossy cup, the slant of light, the roar of the creek, the day of peace between Jesse and me. I would tell her of everything that moved me, every gift received, every lesson learned, for no journey is complete until we carry the stories home.

ELEVEN

SIMPLICITY

THE SPELL OF THE MOUNTAINS began to evaporate as soon as Jesse and I climbed into the rental car at the Wild Basin trail head. The ignition key, the steering wheel, the sun-fried upholstery chafed my skin; the thrum of pavement under the wheels and the press of traffic hustling into Denver chafed my brain. Everything moved too fast. The car felt like a cage on wheels, hurtling along against a gaudy backdrop of dry plains and snow-capped peaks. Never one to stare at scenery through windows, Jesse dived into his book, a thriller about corpses turning up in the alleys of Paris, and he said scarcely a word until we reached the motel. In the morning we would fly home to Indiana, streaking along even more swiftly at thirty thousand feet, sealed away in a more perfect cage, cut off from earth.

The truce between Jesse and me also began to evaporate as soon as we returned to the land of electricity, money, and clocks. His first act on entering our motel room was to switch on the television, and the sound of it was like a file scraping my nerves. I took refuge in the bathroom, figuring that hot water, at least, would be welcome. But the wall-to-wall mirror and the fierce lights quickly unsettled me. After a week of feeling vigorous and fit in the open air, I looked at my grizzled reflection and felt shabby and old.

A shower and shave did not make the television racket any

more bearable. Emerging from the growl of pipes and exhaust fan into the blare of a music video, I snapped at Jesse, "Does that have to be so loud?"

"If you want it off, why don't you say so?" he shot back.

"I only asked you to turn it down."

"You're the boss." He jabbed the remote control and the picture blinked out. "It's all trash anyhow."

I didn't argue, because I could feel the tension rising between us again, like the onset of a fever. Now that we had left the trail I was in charge once more of budget and schedule, and that alone would have irked him. Back in the city, where much of what I saw struck me as wasteful, ugly, or mad, I was also prone to the ranting and lamentation that had cast a shadow over Creation for Jesse. I would have to curb my tongue. I would have to find a way back through this confusion to the sanity and clarity I had felt in the mountains.

We unpacked, and soon our sweaty clothes and camping gear lay in heaps about the room, a room already overstuffed with two queen-size beds, a plywood bureau and desk, matching table and chairs, and half a dozen lamps. The lamps cast a wan light onto walls decorated with vaguely Impressionist views of the French countryside. By opening the heavy curtains at our window I could see, beyond the snarl of billboards and smokestacks and roads, the Rockies glowing serenely in the last light.

I stood there for so long that Jesse came to join me. He gazed quietly for a moment, then let out a deep breath.

"It's hard to believe we were up in those fields of snow only this morning."

"It does seem a long way," I agreed, touching the string of shells and stones at my throat.

I wanted to embrace him, the mountains, the light. But he soon backed away, and we both resumed sorting our gear.

To keep the clutter of the room at bay, and to still the panic I was feeling from the crush of the city outside, I summoned up an image from the mountains: my green poncho, spread out like a tablecloth on the ground, with everything I needed to live comfortably in the woods—clothes, food, fuel, water, tent, sleeping bag, tools—covering no more than a quarter of the fabric. I carried that image with me into sleep.

The Latin word for hope, *sperare*, comes from an Indo-European root, *spei*, which means to expand. You can hear that old root in *prosper*, and you can hear its denial in *despair*. To be hopeful is not only to feel expansive, but to count on an ever-flowing bounty, while to despair is to feel constrained, to fear that the springs of life are drying up.

Try arguing before a chamber of commerce, a board of directors, or a legislature that we should honor limits—on consumption, population, territory, salary, size—and you will discover that the link between hope and growth is not merely etymological, it is visceral. We balk at barriers. Don't fence me in, we sing. We believe in our bones that to have more of anything good is always better than to have less. Get bigger or get out, a Secretary of Agriculture warns farmers. If you're not growing, you're dying, a business guru warns executives. So our cities and houses and budgets and waistlines keep swelling.

I woke at dawn, not to the sounds of creek and birds but to the whine of compressors and the roar of trucks. The air in our motel room was stale. I opened the curtains, but could not open the sealed window. To the northwest, the mountains loomed through a haze of smog, like an afterthought on the horizon. Between here and there lay gas stations, eateries, swarms of houses, an auto auction yard, radio towers, derricks, oil tanks, and one of the largest truck stops I had ever seen: Sapp Bros. Food & Fuel.

Feeling stifled in the room, I went outside for a walk, but there was nowhere to walk except on pavement, dodging traffic. Why all these errands, and the day barely begun? The motel parking lot gave way to a poison-perfect lawn where sprinklers hissed, then the fringe of lawn gave way to concrete. Choosing the least-traveled path, a service road leading into a warehouse district, I shuffled along through beer cans, fast-food wrappers, cast-off mufflers, and skittering newspapers. I had brought along my notebook, hoping to find a bird or flower for sketching, but I saw nothing alive except drivers high in their cabs and a pair of guard dogs, Dobermans, that bared their teeth at me through a chain-link fence. Eventually the pressure of gray buildings and diesel fumes turned me back.

While I drank coffee in the motel lobby, two white-haired men sitting nearby on a plaid couch argued about whether their church could use another Bible class. One man thought the present class was way too big, while the other thought it could use a few more people. "There's so many talkers now," said the first man, "even God can't get a word in edgewise." "But the age we're getting to be," the second man replied, "we need every brain cell we can pack in the room."

As I pulled out my notebook to record their sayings, it fell open to the page I had marked with an aspen leaf, the one listing sources of hope: *Wildness, Beauty, Simplicity, Body Bright, Family, Fidelity, Skill.* Running my mind over the list, as if running my fingers over the necklace of beads, I felt reassured. Even here in the fluorescent glare of the lobby, amidst the buzz of phones and computer printers and hitting-the-road conversations, these words held their promise. The power lay not in the words themselves, but in the stubborn realities to which they pointed. They were tokens of healing energies that we could tap even here, in a hectic city, in the confusion of hasty journeys.

Because Jesse and I, too, needed to hit the road, I closed the notebook and trooped upstairs, to wake him, in a brighter mood than when I had set out.

The item on my list of talismans that seemed most out of keeping with the bustle of departure, and yet most vital as an antidote, was simplicity. Whenever I return from a spell in the woods or waters or mountains, I am dismayed by the noise and jumble of the workaday world. One moment I could lay out everything I need on the corner of a poncho, could tally my responsibilities on the fingers of one hand, and the next moment it seems I couldn't fit all my furniture and tasks into a warehouse. Time in the wilds, like time in the silence of meditation, reminds me how much of what I ordinarily do is mere dithering and how much of what I own is mere encumbrance. The list of urgent jobs I leave on my desk before a journey always looks, on my return, like the jottings of a lunatic. Coming home, I can see there are too many appliances in my cupboards, too many clothes in my closet, too many books on my shelves and files in my drawers, too many dollars in my bank account, too many strings of duty and desire jerking me in too many directions. The opposite of simplicity, as I understand it, is not complexity, but scatter, clutter, weight.

Returning from a journey or surfacing from meditation, I yearn to pare my life down to essentials. I vow to live more simply, by purchasing nothing that I do not really need, by giving away everything that is excess, by refusing all chores that do not arise from my central concerns. I make room for silence. I avoid television, with its blaring novelties, and advertising, with its phony bait. Whenever possible I go about town on bicycle or foot. I resolve to slow down and savor each moment instead of always rushing on into the future.

The simplicity I seek is not the enforced austerity of the poor, which I have seen up close, and which I do not glamorize. I seek instead the richness of a gathered and deliberate life, the richness that comes from letting one's belongings and commitments be few in number and high in quality. I aim to preserve, in my ordinary days, the lightness and purpose that I have discovered on my clarifying journeys.

As our plane banked around after take-off, we caught one last glimpse of the Front Range shining to the west.

"So long, Rockies," Jesse muttered, then returned to his book.

"Have they found out who's killing all those unlucky folks in Paris?" I asked him.

"Not yet," he answered, in a tone that put me on notice he would rather read than talk.

I pressed my cheek against the window. Viewed from the air, Denver seemed to be blundering outward in every direction, without plan or reason, flinging subdivisions and strip malls and roads into the foothills and plains. No doubt many who lived there felt the city was already large enough. But even more people were eagerly joining the sprawl or making fortunes from it, and who was going to stop them? Like other American cities, Denver swells on a blind faith in abundance, a faith that there will always be enough water and land, enough metal and wood, and that oil will always be cheap. While I reflected on the folly of this addiction to growth, cheap oil carried Jesse and me home toward Indiana.

Except for the patchwork of irrigated fields and the green tendrils of waterways, the shortgrass steppes of Colorado were the color of buttermilk pancakes. The plowed fields not yet in crops more nearly matched the color of the airplane wing, a dusky gray like tarnished silver. In these arid lands the drainage patterns branching down from the hills were as clear as the seams on an outdoor face. In western Nebraska and Kansas we began seeing vast circular fields defined by pivoting irrigation equipment—a green that will fade away in thirty or forty years, hydrologists predict, when the Oglala aquifer has been pumped dry. Set within the grid of section lines, these circles look like solar arrays. In fact they *are* solar arrays, turning sunlight into beans or wheat, but clumsy by comparison to the grass that once flourished there without benefit of fertilizers or pesticides or pumps.

From the air, Missouri and Illinois and Indiana appeared to be more densely patterned, with the rectangles of farms and the somber patches of woodlots carved up by housing developments and highways. Buildings clung to the roads, huddled into clumps to form towns, piled into great drifts to make cities. Roads and rails and power lines bound settlement to settlement, radiating into every hollow, slicing through every woods, a net flung over the land.

Gazing down on all of this from six miles in the air, I realized that nothing will halt the spread of human empire, nothing will prevent us from expanding our numbers and our sway over every last inch of earth—nothing except outward disaster or inward conversion. Since I could not root for disaster, I would have to work for a change of heart and mind. The word that came to me, as I flew home from the mountains with my worried son, was *restraint*. Here was a key to the work of healing, as it was also a key to the practice of fidelity. If we hope to survive on this planet, if we wish to leave breathing room for other creatures, we must learn restraint, learn not merely to will it, but to desire it, to say *enough* with relish and conviction.

But how are we to achieve restraint when we seem mindlessly devoted to growth? Increase and multiply, the Lord says, and we do so exuberantly. Like birds and bees and bacteria, we yearn to propagate our kind. Nothing could be more natural. We are unusual among species only in being able to escape, for the short run, the natural constraints on our population and appetites, and in being able to magnify our hungers through the lens of technology.

It seems that our evolutionary history has shaped us to equate well-being with increase, to yearn not merely for more offspring but more of everything, more shoes and meat and horsepower and loot. In a hunting and gathering society—the arena in which our ancestors spent all but the last few thousand years—the fruits of an individual's search for more food, better tools, and richer land were brought back and shared with the tribe. The more relentless the search, the more likely the tribe would be to flourish. As a result of that history, observes anthropologist Lionel Tiger, "We are calculating organisms exquisitely equipped to desire more and truculent and grim about enduring less."

How much any group can accumulate or use is limited, of course, by their level of technology. Hunters on foot armed with stone-tipped weapons can wipe out large, slow-moving creatures, like woolly mammoths and giant beavers; they can open up grasslands by burning; they can alter the mix of plants in their home territory; but they cannot turn a mountain inside out in search of glittering metal or clear-cut a forest or heat up the atmosphere or poison the sea. The harnessing of mechanical power dramatically increased our ability to make the world over to suit ourselves; the rise of towns enabled us to pile up wealth, since we no longer had to haul it from campsite to campsite; and the withering of communal ties allowed more and more of that wealth to be sequestered in private hands. I suspect that we are no more greedy than our ancestors, no more eager for comfort, only far more potent in pursuing our desires.

The constant hankering for more, which served hunting and gathering peoples well, has become a menace in this age of clever machines and burgeoning populations. Our devotion to perpetual growth now endangers the planet, by exhausting resources and accelerating pollution and driving other species to extinction; it upsets community, by severing our links with the past, by outstripping our capacity for change, by swelling the scale of institutions and settlements beyond reach of our understanding; and it harms the individual, by encouraging gluttony, a scramble for possessions, and a nagging discontent even in the midst of plenty.

What are we poor ravenous creatures to do? We may keep riding the exponential curve higher and higher on every graph— widgets produced, oil burned, carbon dioxide released, hamburgers sold, acres paved, trees cut down, soils plowed up, babies born—until nature jerks us back toward the zero point. Or we may choose to live more simply and conservingly, and therefore more sustainably. I doubt that there is anything in our biology to lead us onto the saner, milder path. Biology, I'm afraid, is all on the side of shopping, gluttony, and compulsive growth. If we are to achieve restraint, it will have to come from culture, that shared conversation by which we govern our appetites. Just as our technology and our short-term ability to ignore the constraints of nature distinguish us from other species, so we are also distinguished by the ability to impose limits on ourselves through reason and ritual and mindfulness. The acceptance of limits, in fact, is part of what distinguishes an adult human being from a child.

While I work on this chapter, National Public Radio carries a report about the culling of elephants in a South African game reserve. Animal rights activists protest the killing, but rangers insist that the elephants, having multiplied beyond the land's carrying capacity, are devastating the park by uprooting trees, gouging trails, trampling vegetation, exposing the soil to erosion. In the absence of predators, beaver in our own country can devastate a woods, and deer can graze fragile plants beyond the point of recovery. No matter how intelligent, these animals possess no inborn curb to prevent them from destroying their own habitat. The growth of their populations is checked only by the supply of water or food, by predators and rival species, or by disease.

Many anthropologists now believe that early humans behaved very much like elephants and beaver and deer, degrading one habitat after another, then moving on. As our ancestors spread over the globe, they left deserts and the bones of extinct species in their wake. Such evidence suggests that the ecological wisdom surviving today in remnants of traditional cultures had to be learned over long periods of time, through trial and error. The American landscape is dotted with sites of ancient social experiments that failed, including those of the industrious people who raised great earthworks along the Ohio and Mississippi river valleys in my part of the country. Only gradually did humans, here and there, develop cultural practices—stories and taboos, methods of birth control, rituals for hunting and planting and harvesting, rules about the use of common land—that curbed our instinct to follow the hunger for more wherever it leads.

The capacity for restraint based on knowledge and compassion is a genuine source of hope, though an embattled one. In an effort to clean up the atmosphere, the Environmental Protection Agency recently proposed higher standards for emissions from smokestacks and cars; before the ink was dry on the proposal, governors and industrialists attacked the standards as too expensive, claiming that the richest country in the world cannot afford to pay the real price of energy, nor to cut back on the use of electricity and gasoline, in exchange for breathable air. You can see this pattern repeated over and over in the daily news. One group of citizens calls for a halt to off-shore drilling, the cutting of old-growth timber, the draining of wetlands, the release of greenhouse gases, the building of new highways, or the dumping of toxins into streams, while others call for more drilling, more cutting, more paving, more manufacturing, more more more. For every voice that echoes Thoreau's famous plea, "Simplify, simplify," a dozen cry, "Amplify, amplify!"

As I listened on the car radio to the report about the havoc wrought by elephants, I passed a field where bulldozers grunted and shoved, uprooting a woods to make way for another burger joint. The present scale of human destructiveness is unprecedented, but the impulse to eat whatever is within reach, to manipulate our surroundings, to provide against future scarcity, is entirely natural. While it may be channeled, it cannot be eradicated. What is *un*natural, what comes only from culture, is behavior that arises from knowledge, reflection, and regard for other forms of life. We are the only species capable of exterminating other species wholesale, but we're also the only one capable of acting, through love and reason, to preserve our fellow creatures. We are unique in our ability to affect the fate of the planet, but also unique in our ability to predict those effects and to change our ways in light of what we foresee.

Although I respect the power of biology in shaping our lives, I am not a determinist. If I were, I wouldn't be writing a book about hope. Since our identification of hope with perpetual growth is rooted in our evolutionary history, we can't just decide to feel good about living with less. We cannot force ourselves to welcome limits. We can, however, shift the focus of our expansive desires. We can change, deliberately and consciously, the standard by which we measure prosperity. We can choose to lead a materially simpler life not as a sacrifice but as a path toward fulfillment. In ancient terms, we can learn to seek spiritual rather than material growth.

Religious traditions the world over maintain that one who follows the Way should live simply. Do not lay up treasures on earth, we are told, if you desire treasures in heaven. So Prince Siddhartha and Francis of Assisi leave their fathers' mansions and strip off their fine clothes and walk the roads as beggars. Gandhi eats modestly of vegetables and fruits, sitting cross-legged on the floor in a peasant's hut, wearing a loincloth woven from homespun yarn. A Lakota shaman fasts. Monks dwell in bare cells, hermits in caves, seekers of visions in the open air. Suffering is not the point, although masochists may forget that; the point is to concentrate energy on spiritual work. When Jesus warned that it would be easier for a camel to pass through the eye of a needle than for a rich man to enter the kingdom of heaven, he did not mean, as I read the passage, that wealth is evil, but that the piling up and protection of wealth is all-consuming. The rich man is too preoccupied with being rich to be enlightened or saved.

Meditation, contemplation, pilgrimage, and other forms of religious inquiry are only part of what I mean by "spiritual." I also mean the nourishment that comes to us through art, music, literature, and science, through conversation, through skillful and useful work, through the sharing of bread and stories, through encounters with beauty and wildness. I mean a slowing down and focusing on the present moment, with its inexhaustible depths, rather than a dashing through life toward some ever-retreating goal.

"In the love of money," wrote the eighteenth-century Quaker John Woolman, "business is proposed, then the urgency of affairs push forward, and the mind cannot in this state discern the good and perfect will of God concerning us." One need not believe in God to sense how easily the love of money and the urgency of affairs may crush our inward life. So as to keep himself clear for the inward life and for service to his neighbors, Woolman chose to limit his business by closing a successful store that threatened to absorb all his care, relying instead on a small income from tailoring to support his family: "I saw that an humble man, with the blessing of the Lord, might live on a little, and that where the heart was set on greatness, success in business did not satisfy the craving; but that commonly with an increase of wealth the desire of wealth increased."

Indeed, if we imagine that the greatness we yearn for can be reckoned in dollars or pesos or yen, if we imagine it can be purchased in stores, then there will be no end to our craving, as the drug trade and corporate takeovers and political graft daily remind us. For an image of that insatiable frenzy, visit a casino, watch a game show, or look at brokers on the floor of any stock exchange as they race about and flail their arms and shout, their every gesture signifying *more*. Trucks for a company that refills vending machines in our town bear on their flanks the slogan SATISFACTION AT THE DROP OF A COIN, and billboards for the local mall proclaim SHOP LIKE YOU MEAN IT. But shopping will not give us meaning, and vending machines will not deliver satisfaction. Every time we jump in the car merely for the sake of motion, every time we browse the aisles of stores without needing a thing, or switch on television to banish silence, or surf the Net for distraction, or pump ourselves full of chemicals in search of a jolt, we are hunting for a freshness that we're far more likely to find in the place from which we set out, had we but eyes to see. In the scramble for money and things, we doom ourselves to frustration and we darken our souls.

Already two centuries ago, John Woolman realized that the earth, too, pays a price for our greed: "So great is the hurry in the spirit of this world, that in aiming to do business quickly and to gain wealth the creation at this day doth loudly groan." Thus our needs and the needs of the planet coincide. An outward modesty in dress and shelter and food not only leaves us more time and attention for pursuit of the Way, it also leaves more of the world's bounty for others to enjoy.

Each year the average American consumes roughly thirty times as much of the earth's nonrenewable resources as does the average citizen of India or Mexico. Who most needs to learn restraint? I won't presume to advise the poor how they should order their appetites. As for citizens in prosperous nations, most of us are living nowhere near the edge of survival. This very excess is reason for hope, because it means we could cut back dramatically on our consumption of food and fuel, our use of wood and metal, and on the size of our houses and wardrobes, without suffering any deprivation. We could not only free this surplus for others to use, now and in the future, but we could free ourselves from the burden of lugging it around. Just as we grow fat from eating and drinking too much, so we may grow fit from eating less. As we run ourselves ragged by chasing after too many thrills and tasks, so we may become centered and calm by remaining faithful to a few deep concerns. As we increase the likelihood of strife by scrambling for more wealth, so we may increase the likelihood of peace by living modestly and by sharing what we have.

Less burdened by possessions, less frenzied by activities, we might play more with our children, look after our elders, take walks with our lovers, talk with friends, help neighbors, plant flowers, pick apples, read books, make music, learn to juggle or draw, pursue philosophy or photography, come to know the local trees and birds and rocks, watch clouds, study stars. We might take better care of the land. We might lie down at night and rise up in the morning without feeling the cramp of anxiety. Instead of leaping around like grasshoppers from notion to notion, we might sit still and think in a connected way about our families, our communities, and the meaning of life.

Scientists with a yen for large numbers have calculated that there are more possible paths among the neurons of the brain than there are elementary particles in the universe—hence our capacity for nearly infinite permutations of thought, no matter how bare our closets or calendars. Outward simplicity does not require us to be simple-minded, therefore, nor does it require grim renunciation, but offers instead the promise of elegance and renewal.

For days after reaching home from the Rockies, I felt oppressed by the glut of things, the din of messages, the seethe of machines, the bulk of buildings. My desk was mounded with mail. My floor was littered with unopened parcels. Lights blinked on the answering machine and dozens of requests lurked in the bowels of the computer. Family and friends, students and colleagues, neighbors and strangers marked my return by calling for help. Meanwhile, the basement faucet had sprung a leak, a gutter sagged, the car's engine was tapping ominously, our wildflower patch had all but disappeared under a surf of alien weeds, and grass too high for our tired mower waved in the June sunshine. Despite my yearning for simplicity, the life to which I had returned was over-full of duties and demands.

"You don't have to do everything your first day home," Ruth pointed out to me, as I set to work with my usual fury.

Even though I knew better, I kept imagining that if I could only clear the decks, answer every request, fix every broken thing, *then* I would simplify my life. But trying to catch up once and for all is like digging a hole in sand: no matter how fast you shovel, new sand keeps pouring in. Unable to make any headway, missing the mountains, missing the company of my son, who had been caught up once more in his whirl of teenage friendships, I began to slide down the slope toward gloom.

Familiar with my moods from thirty years of marriage, Ruth kept an eye on me to make sure I didn't slide too far, and also to make sure I didn't throw out any crucial mail or junk the car or put up a FOR SALE sign in the front yard.

One evening that first week home, friends called to invite us out to their farm a few miles west of Bloomington for a look at the stars. Ruth covered the mouthpiece on the phone and told me she thought it would be a shame to squander this clear night.

"I've got too much work to do," I told her, pausing on my way upstairs with an armload of papers.

"You've been working since five o'clock this morning."

"Another few long days and I'll get caught up."

Ruth looked at me hard, then said into the phone, "We'll be there in half an hour."

I knew she was right to drag me away from my chores, so I went along without grumbling. Ruth has always been able to navigate through a maze of possessions without losing her way, and to carry in her mind a hundred tasks without sinking beneath the burden. On our drive into the country, whenever I began to speak about fixing the car or balancing the checkbook, she asked me about our time in the Rockies. So I told her in exuberant detail of quarreling with Jesse and making peace, of rafting through breakneck water on the Cache la Poudre, of snowshoeing up into avalanche country, told her of laying out all my gear on the corner of a green poncho, told her of meeting hummingbird and coyote and elk, told her of watching sunlight pour through the lodgepole pines and of listening all night to the creek.

By the time we rolled down the curving gravel drive to John and Beth's place, the mountain memories had steadied me. We could see our friends walking to meet us over a path of stepping-stones through grass allowed to grow waist-high for the sake of butterflies and birds, their silhouettes tall and thin against a background of stars.

I climbed out of the car with a greeting on my lips, but the sky hushed me. From the black bowl of space countless fiery lights shone down, each one a sun or a swirl of suns, the whole brilliant host of them enough to strike me dumb. The Milky Way arced overhead from Scorpius on the southern horizon to Cassiopeia in the north, reminding me of froth glimmering on the dark surface of North St. Vrain Creek. I knew the names of a dozen constellations and half a dozen of the brightest stars, but I was not thinking in words right then. The deep night drew my scattered pieces back to the center, stripped away all clutter and weight, and set me free.

TWELVE

BEAUTY

No star outshines my daughter. In the weeks and months since Eva's wedding, I have parceled out my joy into its elements, remembering the music, the flowers, the gowns and tuxedos, the friends whispering under the vaulted ceiling of the church. I can see the four grandmothers walking gingerly down the aisle clutching the arms of ushers, Ruth dabbing a handkerchief to her eyes as Jesse leads her to a seat, Jesse beaming and his blond hair newly shorn of dreadlocks gleaming. I see the groomsmen filing out with Matthew to stand expectantly near the altar, Matthew smiling through his beard as he gazes up the aisle for a glimpse of his bride, the bridesmaids in their dresses of midnight blue gathered around the shining face of my daughter.

In memory, I wait beside Eva in the vestibule to play my bit part as father of the bride. She is supposed to remain hidden from the congregation until her queenly entrance, but in her eagerness to see what's going on up front she leans forward to peek around the edge of the half-closed door. The satin roses appliqued to her gown catch the light as she moves, and the toes of her pale silk shoes peep out from beneath the hem. The flower girls watch her every motion. Twins a few days shy of their third birthday, they flounce their unaccustomed frilly skirts, twirl their bouquets, and stare with wide eyes down the great length of carpet leading

139

through the avenue of murmuring people. Eva hooks a hand on my elbow while the bridesmaids fuss over her, fixing the gauzy veil, spreading the long ivory train of her gown, tucking into her bun a loose strand of hair, which glows the color of honey filled with sunlight. Clumsy in my rented finery—patent leather shoes that are a size too small and starched shirt and stiff black tuxedo—I stand among these gorgeous women like a crow among doves. I realize they are gorgeous not because they carry bouquets or wear silk dresses, but because the festival of marriage has slowed time down until any fool can see their glory.

Concerned that we might walk too fast, as we did in rehearsal, Eva demonstrates once more a gliding ballet step to use as we process down the aisle—slide the sole of one shoe forward, bring the feet together, pause; slide, feet together, pause—all in rhythm with the organ.

"It's really simple, Daddy," she says, as I botch it again.

On an ordinary day, I would have learned the step quickly, but this is no ordinary day, and these few furtive seconds of instruction in the vestibule are not enough for my pinched feet. I fear that I will stagger like a wounded veteran beside my elegant daughter.

Eva, meanwhile, seems blissfully confident, not only of being able to walk gracefully, as she could do in her sleep, but of standing before this congregation and solemnly promising to share her life with the man who waits in thinly disguised turmoil at the far end of the aisle. Poised on the dais a step higher than Matthew, below the mystifying wooden cross, wearing a black ministerial robe and a white stole, is the good friend whom Eva and I know best as our guide on canoe trips through the Boundary Waters. He grins so broadly that his full cheeks push up against the round rims of his spectacles.

"There's one happy preacher," Eva says.

"He believes in marriage," I reply.

"So do I. Remember, Matt and I figured out that between you

and Mom and his folks, our parents have been married fifty-eight years."

"So many?" I ask.

"Fifty-eight and counting." Eva lets go of my arm to lift a hand to her throat, touching the string of pearls she has borrowed from Ruth. The necklace was a sixteenth birthday gift to Ruth from her own parents, who have now been married over half a century all by themselves.

Love *can* be durable, I'm thinking, as Eva returns her free hand to my arm and tightens her grip. The arm she holds is my left one, close against my racing heart. On her own left arm she balances a great sheaf of flowers—daisies and lilies, marigolds, snapdragons, bee balm, feverfew—the sumptuous handiwork of a gardening friend, and in her left hand she holds a Belgian lace handkerchief, also borrowed from Ruth, in case she cries. But so far there's no welling of tears in those bold brown eyes.

The organ strikes up Bach's "Jesu, Joy of Man's Desiring" for the bridesmaids' entrance, and down the aisle they skim, those gorgeous women in midnight blue. The organist is another friend, the former choir director of our church, an old pro whose timing and touch are utterly sure, and likewise a generous man, who has postponed open heart surgery until next week in order to play for Eva's wedding. He tilts his head back to read the music through bifocals, then tilts it forward to study the progress of the bridesmaids, then tilts it back again as he raises the volume a notch for the entrance of the flower girls. Overawed by the crowd, the twins hang back until their mother nudges them along and they spy their father waving eagerly at them from the third row of seats, and then they dash and skip, carrying their fronds of flowers like spears.

Finally, only the bride and the father of the bride remain in the vestibule. Eva whispers, "Remember, now, don't walk too fast." But how can I walk slowly while my heart races? I have forgotten the ballet step she tried to show me. I want events to pause so that

I can practice the step, so that we can go canoeing once more in the wilderness, so that we can sit on a boulder by the sea and talk over life's mysteries, so that I can make up to my darling for anything she may have lacked in her girlhood.

But events do not pause. The organ sounds the first few bars of Purcell's "Trumpet Voluntary," our cue to show ourselves. We move into the open doorway, and two hundred faces turn their lit eyes on us. Eva tilts her face up at me, quirks the corners of her lips into a tight smile, and says, "Here we go, Daddy." And so, lifting our feet in unison, we go.

The wedding took place here in Bloomington, hometown for Matthew as well as Eva, on a sizzling Saturday in July. Now, as I write in early September, not quite two months later, I can summon up hundreds of details from that radiant day, but on the day itself I was aware only of a surpassing joy. The red glow of happiness had to cool before it would crystallize into memory.

Pardon my cosmic metaphor, but I can't help thinking of the physicists' claim that, if we trace the universe back to its origins in the Big Bang, we find the multiplicity of things fusing into greater and greater simplicity, until at the moment of creation itself there is only pure undifferentiated energy. Without being able to check their equations, I think the physicists are right. I believe the energy they speak of is holy, by which I mean it is the closest we can come with our instruments to measuring the strength of God. I also believe this primal energy continues to feed us, directly through the goods of Creation, and indirectly through the experience of beauty. The thrill of beauty is what entranced me as I stood with Eva's hand hooked over my arm while the wedding march played, as it entrances me on these September nights when I walk over dewy grass among the songs of crickets and stare at the Milky Way.

We are seeing the Milky Way, and every other denizen of the sky, far more clearly these days thanks to the sharp eyes of the

Hubble Space Telescope, as it orbits out beyond the blur of Earth's atmosphere. From data beamed down by the telescope, for example, I can summon onto my computer screen an image of Jupiter wrapped in its bands of cloud like a ball of heathery yarn. Then I view the planet after meteor fragments have burned a series of holes, like dark stepping-stones, in the frothy atmosphere. Next I call up the Cat's Eye Nebula, with its incandescent swirls of red looped around the gleam of a helium star, for all the world like the burning iris of a tiger's eye. This fierce glare began its journey toward earth three thousand years ago, about the time my Assyrian ancestors were in their prime and busy carving reliefs of a lion hunt to honor a bloodthirsty king. Pushing back deeper in time and farther in space, I summon onto my screen the Eagle Nebula, seven thousand light-years away, a trio of dust clouds upraised like rearing horses, their dark bodies scintillating with the sparks of newborn stars. I study images of quasars giving birth to galaxies, galaxies whirling in the shapes of pinwheels, supernovas ringed by strands of luminous debris, immense tornados of hot gas spiraling into black holes; and all the while I'm delving back and back toward that utter beginning when you and I and my daughter and her new husband and the bright heavenly host were joined in the original burst of light.

On these cool September mornings, I have been poring over two sets of photographs, those from deep space and those from Eva's wedding album, trying to figure out why such different images— of supernova and shining daughter, of spinning galaxies and trembling bouquets—set up in me the same hum of delight. The feeling is unusually intense for me just now, so soon after the nuptials, but it has never been rare. As far back as I can remember, things seen or heard or smelled, things tasted or touched, have provoked in me an answering vibration. The stimulus might be the sheen of moonlight on the needles of a white pine, or the iridescent glimmer on a dragonfly's tail, or the lean silhouette of a ladder-back chair, or the glaze on a hand-thrown pot. It might be bird song or a Bach cantata or the purl of water over stone. It might be a line of poetry, the outline of a cheek, the arch of a ceiling, the savor of bread, the sway of a bough or a bow. The provocation might be as grand as a mountain sunrise or as humble as an icicle's jeweled tip, yet in each case a familiar surge of gratitude and wonder wells up in me.

Now and again some voice raised on the stairs leading to my study, some passage of music, some noise from the street, will stir a sympathetic thrum from the strings of the guitar that tilts against the wall behind my door. Just so, over and over again, impulses from the world stir a responsive chord in me—not just any chord, but a particular one, combining notes of elegance, exhilaration, simplicity, and awe. The feeling is as recognizable to me, as unmistakable, as the sound of Ruth's voice or the beating of my own heart. A screech owl calls, a comet streaks the night sky, a story moves unerringly to a close, a child lays an arrowhead in the palm of my hand, a welder installs a pair of railings on our front steps, my daughter smiles at me through her bridal veil, and I feel for a moment at peace, in place, content. I sense in those momentary encounters a harmony between myself and whatever I behold. The word that seems to fit most exactly this feeling of resonance, this sympathetic vibration between inside and outside, is *beauty*.

What am I to make of this resonant feeling? Do my sensory thrills tell me anything about the world? Does beauty reveal a kinship between my small self and the great cosmos, or does my desire for meaning only fool me into thinking so? Perhaps, as biologists maintain, in my response to patterns I am merely obeying the old habits of evolution. Perhaps, like my guitar, I am only a sounding box played on by random forces.

I must admit that two cautionary sayings keep echoing in my head, as they may well be echoing in yours. "Beauty is only skin deep," I've heard repeatedly, and "Beauty is in the eye of the beholder." Like most proverbs, these two convey partial truths that are commonly mistaken for the whole truth. Appealing surfaces may hide ugliness, true enough, as many a handsome villain or femme fatale should remind us. Some of the prettiest butterflies and mushrooms and frogs are also the most poisonous. It is equally true that our taste may be influenced by our upbringing, by training, by cultural fashion. One of my neighbors plants in his yard a pink flamingo made of translucent plastic and a concrete goose dressed in overalls, while I plant in my yard oxeye daisies and jack-in-the-pulpits and maidenhair ferns, and both of us, by our own lights, are chasing beauty. The women of one tribe scarify their cheeks, and the women of another tribe paint their cheeks with rouge, while the women of a third tribe hide their cheeks behind veils, each obeying local notions of loveliness.

Mustn't beauty be shallow if it can be painted on? Mustn't beauty be a delusion if it can blink off and on like a flickering bulb? A wedding gown will eventually grow musty in a mothproof box, flowers will fade, and the glow will seep out of the brightest day. I'll grant that we may be fooled by facades, we may be deceived by fashion, we may be led astray by our fickle eyes. But I have been married to Ruth for thirty years, remember. I've watched Eva grow for twenty-four years, Jesse for twenty, and these loved ones have taught me another possibility. Season after season I have knelt over fiddleheads breaking ground, have studied the wings of swallowtails nectaring on blooms, have spied skeins of geese high in the sky. There are books I have read, pieces of music I have listened to, ideas I have revisited time and again with fresh delight. I have lived among enough people whose beauty runs all the way through, I have been renewed by enough places and creatures, I have fed long enough from certain works of intellect and imagination, to feel absolutely certain that genuine beauty is more than skin deep, that real beauty dwells not in my own eye alone but out in the world.

While I can speak with confidence of what I feel in the presence of beauty, I must go out on a speculative limb if I am to speak about the qualities in the world that call it forth. Far out on that limb, therefore, let me suggest that a creature, an action, a landscape, a line of poetry or music, a scientific formula, or anything else that might seem beautiful, seems so because it gives us a glimpse of the underlying order of things. The swirl of a galaxy and the swirl of a gown resemble one another not merely by accident, but because they follow the grain of the universe. That grain runs through our own depths. What we find beautiful accords with our most profound sense of how things *ought* to be. Ordinarily, we live in a tension between our perceptions and our desires. When we encounter beauty, that tension vanishes, and outward and inward images agree.

Before I climb out any farther onto this limb, let me give biology its due. It may be that in pursuing beauty we are merely obeying our genes. It may be that the features we find beautiful in men or women, in landscape or weather, even in art and music and story, are ones that improved the chances of survival for our ancestors. Put the other way around, it's entirely plausible that the early humans who did *not* tingle at the sight of a deer, the smell of a thunderstorm, the sound of running water, or the stroke of a hand on a shapely haunch, all died out, carrying with them their oblivious genes.

Who can doubt that biology, along with culture, plays a crucial role in tuning our senses? The gravity that draws a man and woman together, leading each to find the other ravishing, carries with it a long history of sexual selection, one informed by a shrewd calculation of fertility and strength. I remember how astonished I was to realize, one rainy spring day in seventh grade, that the girl sitting in the desk beside me was suddenly, enormously *interesting*. My attention was riveted on Mary Kay's long blond hair, which fell in luxuriant waves over the back of her chair until it brushed against a rump that swelled, in a way I had never noticed before, her green plaid skirt. As a twelve-year-old, I would not have called Mary Kay beautiful, although I realize now that is what she was. And I would have balked at the suggestion that my caveman ancestors had any say in my dawning desire, although now I can hear their voices grunting, Go for the lush hair, the swelling rump.

If we take a ride through the suburbs of my city or yours, and study the rolling acres of lawn dotted with clumps of trees and occasional ponds, what do we see but a faithful simulation of the African savannah where humans first lived? Where space and zoning laws permit, the expanse of green will often be decorated by grazing animals, docile and fat, future suppers on the hoof. The same combination of watering holes, sheltering trees, and open grassland shows up in paintings and parks the world over, from New Delhi to New York. It is as though we shape our surroundings to match an image, coiled in our DNA, of the bountiful land.

Perhaps in every case, as in our infatuation with lover or landscape, a sense of biological fitness infuses the resonant, eager, uplifting response to the world that I am calling beauty. Yet I persist in believing there is more to this tingle than an evolutionary reflex. Otherwise, how could a man who is programmed to lust after every nubile female nonetheless be steadily attracted, year after year, to the same woman? Why would I plant my yard with flowers that I cannot eat? Why would I labor to make these sentences fit my thoughts, and why would you labor to read them?

"Beauty is not a means," says Eudora Welty, "not a way of furthering a thing in the world. It is a result; it belongs to ordering, to form, to aftereffect." She is talking here about the writing of fiction, but I think her words apply to any human art. As far back as we can trace our ancestors, we find evidence of a passion for design—decorations on pots, beads on clothes, pigments on the ceilings of caves. Bone flutes have been found at human sites dating back more than thirty thousand years. So we answer the magnificent breathing of the land with our own measured breath; we answer the beauty we find with the beauty we make. Our ears may be finely tuned for detecting the movements of predators or prey, but that does not go very far toward explaining why we should be so moved by listening to Gregorian chants or Delta blues. Our eyes may be those of a slightly reformed ape, trained for noticing whatever will keep skin and bones intact, but that scarcely explains why we should be so enthralled by the lines of a Shaker chair or a Durer engraving, or by photographs of meteor impacts on Jupiter.

As it happens, Jupiter is the brightest light in the sky on these September evenings, blazing in the southeast at dusk. Such a light must have dazzled our ancestors long before telescopes began to reveal the planet's husk of clouds or its halo of moons. We know that night watchers in many cultures kept track of the heavenly dance because the records of their observations have come down to us, etched in stone or inked on papyrus or stitched into stories. Did they watch so faithfully because they believed the stars and planets controlled their fate, or because they were mesmerized by the majesty of the night? I can't speak for them. But when I look at Jupiter, with naked eye or binoculars or in the magnified images broadcast down from the Hubble Telescope, I am not looking for a clue to the morning's weather or to the mood of a deity, any more than I am studying the future of my genes when I gaze at my daughter. I am looking for the sheer bliss of looking.

In the wedding scene that has cooled into memory, I keep glancing at Eva's face as we process down the aisle, trying to match my gawky stride to her graceful one. The light on her skin shimmers through the veil. A ripple of voices follows us toward the altar, like the sound of waves breaking on cobbles. The walk seems to go on forever, but it also seems to be over far too soon. Ready or not, we take our place at center stage, with the bridesmaids to our left, Matthew and his groomsmen to our right. My heart thrashes like a bird in a sack.

The minister gives us both a steadying glance. Then he lifts his voice to inquire of the hushed congregation, "Who blesses this marriage?"

I swallow to make sure my own voice is still there, and say loudly, "The families give their blessing."

I step forward, lift Eva's hand from my arm and place it on Matthew's, a gesture that seemed small in rehearsal yesterday but that seems huge today. Then I climb onto the dais and walk to the lectern, look out over the sea of friends, and read a poem celebrating marriage. The words hover in the air a moment, then are gone.

Now my bit part is over. I leave the stage, carefully stepping around the long train of Eva's dress, and go to my seat beside Ruth, who still dabs a handkerchief to her eyes. I grasp her free hand, so deft and familiar. Thirty years after my own wedding, I want to marry her all over again. Despite my heart's mad thrashing, I have not felt like crying until this moment, as I sit here beside my own bride, while Eva recites her vows with a sob in her throat. When I hear that sob, tears rise in me, but joy rises more swiftly.

Judging from the scientists I know, including Eva and Ruth, and those whom I have read about, you cannot pursue the laws of nature very long without bumping into beauty. "I don't know if it's the same beauty you see in the sunset," a friend tells me, "but it *feels* the same." This friend is a theoretical physicist who has spent a long career deciphering, with pencil and paper and brain, what must be happening in the interior of stars. He recalls for me his thrill on grasping for the first time Dirac's equations describing quantum mechanics, or those of Einstein describing relativity. "They're so beautiful," he says, "you can see immediately they have to be true. Or at least on the way toward truth." I ask him what makes a theory beautiful, and he replies, "Simplicity, symmetry, elegance, and power."

When Einstein was asked how he would have felt had the predictions arising from his equations not been confirmed, he answered that he would have pitied the Creator for having failed to make the universe as perfect as mathematics said it could be. Of course, his predictions were confirmed. Experiments revealed that light does indeed bend along the curvature of space, time slows down for objects traveling near the speed of light, and mass transmutes into energy.

Why nature should conform to theories we find beautiful is far from obvious. The most incomprehensible thing about the universe, as Einstein said, is that it *is* comprehensible. How unlikely, that a short-lived biped on a two-bit planet should be able to gauge the speed of light, lay bare the structure of an atom, or calculate the gravitational tug of a black hole. We are a long way from understanding everything, but we do understand a great deal about how nature behaves. Generation after generation, we puzzle out formulas, test them, and find, to an astonishing degree, that nature agrees. A welder opens the valve on his acetylene torch and strikes a spark, foreseeing the burst of flame. An architect draws designs on flimsy paper, and her buildings stand up through earthquakes. We launch a satellite into orbit and use it to bounce our messages from continent to continent. The machine on which I write these words embodies a thousand insights into the workings of the material world, insights that are confirmed by every tap of the keys, every burst of letters on the screen. My vision is fuzzy, but I view the screen clearly through plastic lenses, their curvature obeying the laws of optics first worked out in detail by Isaac Newton.

By discerning patterns in the universe, Newton believed, he was tracing the hand of God. Even in our secular age, scientists who ponder the origin of things still sometimes appeal to religious language, as when Stephen Hawking concludes *A Brief*

History of Time by proposing that a complete theory of the universe would enable us to "know the mind of God." Although you will find more than half a dozen references to God in Hawking's last chapter, you will not find that name in the index. It is as if the Creator were an embarrassing visitor to a cosmos supposedly ruled by logic and accident.

The dilemma for science is neatly summed up in remarks made by another physicist, Dennis Sciama, who said in an interview, "It's true that people have, internally, a religious feeling, which they use the word God to express, but how can a feeling inside of you tell you that a thing made the whole universe?" How indeed? Divinity won't register on meters. It leaves no track in the eye of the telescope. "The word God," Sciama adds, "just doesn't denote any structure." Little wonder, then, that scientists in our day have largely abandoned the notion of a Creator as an unnecessary hypothesis, or at least an untestable one. While they share Newton's faith that the universe is ruled everywhere by a coherent set of rules, they cannot say, as scientists, how these particular rules came to govern things. You can do science without believing in a divine Legislator, but not without believing in laws.

I spent my teenage years scrambling up the mountain of mathematics, aiming one day to read the classic papers of Einstein and Dirac with comprehension. During my college summers, as I sat on a forklift in a Louisiana factory between trips to the warehouse with loaded crates, I often worked problems in calculus on the backs of shipping pads. Men passing by would sometimes pause to study my scribbles. When they asked what I was doing, I said, Just messing around. I couldn't bring myself to admit that I was after the secrets of the universe. My visitors would frown or grin, baffled, and josh me about having my head stuck way up there in the clouds.

I never rose as high as the clouds. Midway up the slope of mathematics I staggered to a halt, gasping in the rarefied air, well before I reached the heights where the equations of Einstein and Dirac would have made sense. Nowadays I add, subtract, multiply, and do long division when no calculator is handy, and I can do algebra and geometry, and even trigonometry in a pinch, but that is about all that I have kept from the language of numbers. Still, I remember glimpsing patterns in mathematics that seemed as bold and beautiful as a skyful of stars on a clear night.

I am never more aware of the limitations of language than when I try to describe beauty. Language can create its own loveliness, of course, but it cannot deliver to us the radiance we apprehend in the world, any more than a photograph can capture the stunning swiftness of a hawk or the withering power of a supernova. Eva's wedding album holds only a faint glimmer of the wedding itself. All that pictures or words can do is gesture beyond themselves toward the fleeting glory that stirs our hearts. So I keep gesturing.

"All nature is meant to make us think of paradise," Thomas Merton observed. Because Creation puts on a nonstop show, beauty is free and inexhaustible, but we need training in order to perceive more than the most obvious kinds. Even fifteen billion years or so after the Big Bang, echoes of that event still linger in the form of background radiation. Just so, I believe, the experience of beauty is an echo of the order and power that permeate the universe. To measure background radiation, we need subtle instruments; to measure beauty, we need alert intelligence and our five keen senses.

The word *aesthetic* derives from a Greek root meaning sensitive, which derives in turn from a verb meaning to perceive. The more sensitive we are, the more we may be nourished by what Robinson Jeffers called "the astonishing beauty of things." Anyone can take delight in a face or a flower. You need training, however, to perceive the beauty in mathematics or physics or chess, in the architecture of a tree, the design of a bird's wing, or the shiver of breath through a flute. For most of human history, that training has come from elders who taught the young how to pay attention. By paying attention we learn to savor all sorts of patterns, from quantum mechanics to patchwork quilts.

Again, this predilection brings with it a clear evolutionary advantage, for the ability to recognize patterns helped our ancestors to select mates, find food, avoid predators. But this applies to all species, and yet we alone compose symphonies and crossword puzzles, carve stone into statues, map time and space. Have we merely carried our animal need for shrewd perception to an absurd extreme? Or have we stumbled onto a deep congruence between the structure of our minds and the structure of the universe?

I am persuaded the latter is true. I am convinced there is more to beauty than biology, more than cultural convention. It flows around and through us in such abundance, and in such myriad forms, as to exceed by a wide margin any mere evolutionary need. Which is not to say that beauty has nothing to do with survival: I think it has everything to do with survival. Beauty feeds us from the same source that created us. It reminds us of the shaping power that reaches through the flower stem and through our own hands. It restores our faith in the generosity of nature. By giving us a taste of the kinship between our own small minds and the great Mind of the Cosmos, beauty reassures us that we are exactly and wonderfully made for life on this glorious planet, in this magnificent universe. I find in that affinity a profound source of meaning and hope. A universe so prodigal of beauty may actually *need* us to notice and respond, may need our sharp eyes and brimming hearts and teeming minds, in order to close the circuit of Creation.

THIRTEEN

THE WAY OF
THINGS

EVERY TOKEN OF HOPE THAT I'VE GATHERED in my medicine bundle carries a whiff of the holy. If I trace beauty or wildness or the body's own vigor back to their source, I find myself edging toward the wellspring of the sacred. Even the distinctly human measures of hope, such as family and fidelity and simplicity and skill, draw power from nonhuman depths. To speak honestly of my reasons for living in hope, therefore, I must dive into those depths. I must overcome my reluctance, indeed my fear, and say as clearly as language allows what I have come to believe about the Creator.

"Discussing God is not the best use of our energy," warns the Buddhist monk Thich Nhat Hanh, a warning that I bear soberly in mind. More than enough talk has already been uttered in the name of God, Yahweh, Allah, Brahma, Tao, and the many other aliases for the creative power at the heart of things. Some of that talk is wise, some is dangerous, and much of it is arrogant babble. I am wary of adding my own voice to the hubbub. What do I know about the underlying mystery that we call by so many hallowed names? I may speak with some authority of my backyard, my town, or the hill country of southern Indiana. But what do I know of the Ground of Being? Precious little, I confess. Yet every path I take in my hunt for hope leads me toward this murky and risky terrain. In venturing there I may get lost, I may blunder or blaspheme, I may settle for talk about the sacred when only direct experience really counts. What I say about the holy may scare away those readers who are convinced they already possess reliable maps to the realm of spirit, as well as those who are convinced there is no such realm. In spite of the risks, if I am to explain why I live in hope, I must describe my vision of the ultimate reality that sustains and informs everything we do.

From early childhood until I was ten years old, I could have spoken confidently of God as a gentle, giant father in the sky, who looked out for me in the daylight and kept the goblins away in the dark. My days were long and easy; my nights were short and dreamless. At bedtime I prayed with a certainty that God would ease whatever ache I felt, then I closed my eyes, lay still, and a moment later it was morning. Night and day, this reliable God wrapped me in love and filled my body with breath.

Then, during my tenth summer, I went to the hospital for what was supposed to have been routine surgery. My mother assured me that God would go with me into the operating room and hold me in his hand, and when it was over he would carry me back home and mend all that had gone wrong inside of me. Although I trembled, I believed her, right up to the last moment of innocence, when I lay on the table under fierce lights while strangers in blue cloth hats gazed down at me and someone pressed a rubber mask over my nose and mouth, and I breathed in the sweet gas.

What came after was more terrible than anything my fumbling words could grasp. I was floating in a black void, an endless night without moon or stars, when suddenly a huge voice, hate-filled and furious, began roaring in my ears. Out of the darkness loomed the glowing shape of a capital *I*, at first only a bright streak, like a letter fallen from a neon sign, then growing larger and brighter until it filled the world and burned with the menacing red of steel in a blacksmith's forge. Suddenly a great sledge-hammer, like the one my father used to drive fenceposts, came banging down on the fiery *I*, and every clanging blow slammed through me. This went on, it seemed, for longer than I had been alive, the banging and roaring, the fury and fire.

When I swam up out of the anesthesia, knowing nothing of ether nightmares, I could tell from the whispering voices and the drawn faces in the recovery room that I had nearly died. No one confessed this to me until months later, but I gathered from the whispers that I had lost a lot of blood during the operation, nearly too much. Instead of going home in a day or two, I stayed in the hospital more than a week, most of the time flat on my back with my arms strapped down to keep me from tearing at the bandages and tubes. When I was finally permitted to get out of bed, I needed help even to stand up. I shivered in the nurses' arms. Before the operation I had run and jumped and climbed with no thought of my body, but now I had to learn all over again how to walk.

I had also forgotten how to fall asleep. Or rather, in the hospital and then at home, I lay awake brooding for the first time on what sleep might mean. What if the roaring and banging and burning seized me again, and never let go? What if I sank down into the darkness and never found my way back up to the light? What if sleep went on forever?

With its drugged nightmare and its taste of death, the operation was a small agony, as human suffering goes, but it changed me, as if I really had been a slab of red-hot steel reshaped under the blows of a hammer. I lost entirely my childhood confidence in God as a gentle giant who cradled me in the palm of his hand. Had I been older I might have reasoned that a loving power did, after all, reach down and pluck me from the jaws of death. But as a child of ten I could only wonder how I had slipped into those terrible jaws. What had I done to bring on such pain? Bewildered by my brush with death, I could imagine only two explanations: either God was not in charge or God was cruel.

I came to dread the night. I would lie awake for hours, clinging to consciousness. My father and mother took turns singing me songs, telling me stories, soothing me. But after they tiptoed out of my bedroom I opened my eyes and stared at the wedge of light falling through the half-open door. So long as I held onto the light I would be safe. If I let go I might sink into nightmare, for the roaring and pounding awaited me in the darkness. The effort of staring at the light made my eyes burn and my legs twitch. I tried to keep quiet, but my jerking limbs rustled the sheets, and when fear filled me to the brim I sat up in bed and cried out. Soon Mother would come to me, always Mother, for my father soon lost patience with a boy who could not go to sleep without whimpering. She hummed lullabies, or merely sat beside the bed and stroked my hair until weariness finally pulled down the lids of my eyes.

This went on for months, night after night. In rural Ohio, in 1956, in a family without any spare money, nobody thought of taking me to a therapist. Mother did take me to see our minister, a white-haired and quiet-spoken man who left his dairy farm every Sunday to preach at our crossroads Methodist church. We sat in rocking chairs on his front porch. I stared down at my shoes while Mother told him of my troubles, my midnight fears, my doubts. The minister gave me a list of Bible verses that would ease my dread. Before we left he pressed a hand to my forehead, saying, "God loves you, Scott. As sure as you're sitting there." I wanted to believe him, but I no longer could. Whatever power lay behind things, there was more to it than love.

No matter how secure our beginnings, no matter how pampered or lucky we might be, sooner or later all of us go under the hammer of suffering. What pounds us may be humiliation or fever, hunger or cold, a mother's drinking or a father's fist. The shock of the blow forces us to enlarge our view of the world, to make room for the fact of our vulnerability. It may drive us into a shell, make us defensive, even cruel; or it may jolt us into recognizing that others, too, are vulnerable, and thereby deepen our compassion. I tell about a boy's minor surgery and its aftermath not because they rate high on the scale of suffering, but because, in giving me a foretaste of death, they compelled me to examine the foundations of life.

Eventually I learned how to still my twitching legs, how to stifle my cries, so that my parents thought I had overcome the terror of the operation. But the nightmares went on for half a dozen years, until I was well into high school.

Meanwhile, forlorn and frightened, I set about investigating God. I scoured the woods and fields and roads, studied the faces of friends and strangers, watched the sky, looking for clues. What sort of world was this? How did it all hang together? Where had it come from and where was it going? And who or what was running the show? What was my life, or any life, that could so easily be snatched away? It was as though I had suddenly awakened to the strangeness of things.

Like a good Protestant boy, in my search for God I consulted the family Bible, a heavy, leather-bound volume that lay on a maple desk in the living room. Since the Bible was not to be moved from its place of honor, I would stand there at the desk, open to one of the verses from the minister's list, and read a passage over and over until I had it memorized.

> Yea, though I walk through the valley
>   of the shadow of death,
> I will fear no evil:
>   for thou art with me;
> thy rod and thy staff
>   they comfort me.

I was comforted merely to learn that the Psalmist had passed through the shadow of death and lived to sing of it. Recalling the sudden weakness of my legs in the hospital, I was reassured by Isaiah's promise:

> They that wait upon the Lord
>> shall renew their strength;
> they shall mount up with wings as eagles;
>> they shall run and not be weary;
> and they shall walk, and not faint.

The words rolled in my mouth like ripe cherries. I read all the soothing words, including John's famous condensation of the gospel into one sentence: "For God so loved the world, that he gave his only begotten Son, that whosoever believeth in him should not perish, but have everlasting life." I worked my way through the minister's list, learning verses by the dozens, all of them antidotes to doubt.

If I had stuck to those comforting passages I might have regained my old confidence in God. But on my twelfth birthday, Mother's stepmother from Chicago swooped down for a visit in her white Cadillac and feathered hat, and presented me with my very own Bible, a zippered copy of the King James version. Not realizing what a dangerous gift this was, I carried it to my room that night, drew back the zipper to reveal the red-edged pages, turned to the opening lines of Genesis, and started reading. Over the following months I plowed straight on through to the Revelation of John. I never understood more than half of what I read, but that did not slow me down, I was so intent on searching out this Yahweh, this God, this Lord whose book had come to me like a challenge.

The God I found in those closely printed pages was a scary mixture of friend and foe, comforter and tyrant. Here was a king that would scorn his subjects, taunt them, hurl them down into Sheol. Here was a creator who would drown all but a handful of his creatures, then promise not to do it again. Here was a ruler of the universe that would kick Adam and Eve out of the garden, turn a woman to salt, trap a man inside a whale, urge one tribe to slaughter another one, kill every newborn son in a whole country, visit plagues and famine and fire on his enemies. This God of the Bible toyed with people the way our barn cats teased mice. Could the Almighty really be such a bully?

Aside from my sleepless misery following the operation, there was plenty of evidence in my own neighborhood for such a callous God. During the months when I was poring over those red-rimmed pages, a husband in a nearby house often beat his wife and children so hard that I could hear their screams. Another house on our road burned down when the father fell asleep smoking, and afterwards his family shuffled around barefoot in the ashes. Every third or fourth house was poisoned by drink. Driving home with a carload of presents for Christmas, the wife of our grade school janitor was crushed by a gravel truck. In school, a simpleminded boy with flame-red hair was taunted by the other kids until he tumbled to the floor with seizures. Animals died every day on our road, flattened under the tires of cars. More animals died for our food. If our neighborhood was a fair sample of the world, then God seemed not to care how much his creatures suffered.

Having studied that dangerous book from cover to cover, I found I had to choose: either the universe was run by a fickle, fatal, sometimes vicious dictator, or else the Bible did not tell the whole story. I chose the latter. The whole story, I came to believe, was likelier to be told by science.

My infatuation with science had begun much earlier, but it turned into a passion at about the same time I lost my faith in the kindliness of God. The month of my twelfth birthday, which brought me the zippered Bible, was also the October when the Russians launched the first artificial satellite into orbit. I remember hearing over the radio the signals beamed down from Sputnik I, like the chirping of crickets in the autumn fields. However worried the grown-ups might have been by this proof of Soviet wizardry, it lifted my heart, because rockets and satellites promised to carry our questions out into the heavens. Where did the universe come from? Is anyone or anything in charge? Why are we here, alive and thinking? Are we going anywhere, or are we just wandering around, passing the time until we die? And when we die, is that the end, or does some part of us survive?

For years, right on through high school and college and well into my twenties, I believed that science might answer those questions. I read about fossils and fire, neurons and neutrons, quasars and quarks. I performed earnest, clumsy experiments in our garage, using batteries and beakers and a witch's brew of chemicals, and later, older, I performed more careful experiments in laboratories using subtle instruments. I hung around telescopes and cyclotrons. Hungry for order, I memorized star charts and the periodic table of the elements. Given time enough, I figured, chemistry would puzzle out the secret of thought, biology would uncover the springs of life, physics would probe outward to the circumference and inward to the center of things. Then we would know for sure whether the fact of Creation implies a Creator, whether life has a purpose or the universe has a plan, whether mind is more than a fever in matter, whether we have souls.

The story I learned from all of that study is an enthralling one, as grand as any myth. In bare outline, it goes like this: Our universe began in the void with a burst of energy, between ten and twenty billion years ago, and it has been expanding, proliferating new forms, and cooling down ever since. Among the forms congealing out of energy and dust were galaxies like the Milky Way and stars like our sun and planets like Earth. And on this one planet, at least, and most likely on countless others throughout space, matter coalesced into organisms that could reproduce themselves. These organisms in turn gave rise, through gradual small changes and the rigors of survival, to millions upon millions of new living forms, many of them short-lived, some of them durable, all of them capable of sensing, in however modest a fashion, some portion of the universe. To varying degrees, the more complex organisms developed an inward space for thinking and feeling. And in at least one species, our own, that space has grown so large that we can entertain the crazy ambition of comprehending the whole universe.

If that is a more convincing tale than any of those offered by scriptures, as I believe it is, what are we to make of it? "Let us interrogate the great apparition, that shines so peacefully around us," Emerson advised. "Let us inquire, to what end is nature?" We have inquired, with breathtaking ingenuity, and all that we can say, in ever finer detail, is how the apparition seems to work. We are no closer to understanding how this apparition came to be, why it obeys such a peculiar set of rules, and where, if anywhere, it may be going. There seems to be an unbridgeable gulf between all that we can measure with our instruments and the fundamental reality that gives rise to the universe.

The limits of what science can tell us might be summed up in a line I have quoted in an earlier book, from a Nobel laureate in physics, Steven Weinberg: "The more the universe seems comprehensible, the more it also seems pointless." While many scientists would no doubt take issue with Weinberg, insisting that the universe does indeed have a purpose, they would not be able to justify their beliefs by the methods of science. No one has devised an experiment that would reveal what, if anything, the whole show means, and no one is likely to do so.

Much as I still love science, I no longer expect it to answer my deepest questions. Those questions have stayed with me since childhood, and they have nagged at me throughout my hunt for hope. As I have reckoned up the powers and gifts that might help us to solve the tremendous problems we face, again and again I have found myself driven to think about the cosmic setting in which we act. Are we alone, without guidance, in a mindless whirl of atoms? Or is it possible that behind all we see, behind the turmoil and cruelty and loss, there is a mind, a being, a way of things, which we might dimly perceive, and with which we might align our lives? And if there is such a cosmic Way, does it merely set the parameters for what is possible, as gravity limits the motions of planets, or does it offer us help? Are we allied to something infinite and immortal, some Ground of Being that might inform and support our best efforts?

Our answers to those questions will have a profound effect on how we lead our lives. "The significance—and ultimately the quality—of the work we do is determined by our understanding of the story in which we are taking part," as Wendell Berry observes. Even if one accepts, as I do, that the scientific account of the universe is the most convincing story we have so far, one still must decide whether the story has any meaning, and whether we have any role to play in it. If cosmic evolution is only a chain of accidents, then we are free to pursue any goal that pleases us; if, on the other hand, cosmic evolution embodies a plot or purpose, then we had better do all we can to decipher it. We should be skeptical of anyone who claims to know for certain what the meaning of the universe is, but we should be equally skeptical of anyone who claims to know for certain that it has no meaning.

So what do we make of the cosmic story? Is it the tale of an idiot, full of sound and fury, signifying nothing? Is it the record of a divine plan? Is it a grand experiment whose outcome we might influence? However we answer, whether we deny or affirm that there is a Way of things, we must make a leap of faith. Our faith ought to be informed by the best knowledge we can gather— from the testimony of others who have thought hard about these matters, from science and religion, from history and literature, and from our own deepest intuitions—but finally, in trying to make sense of the cosmic story, we must go beyond what can be known for certain. And so, armed with the little knowledge I have gathered in a brief and hectic life, I make my leap.

·　　·　　·

I believe that Creation is holy. It is worthy of our wonder, our study, our devotion and love. It is the work of a Creator whom we can apprehend directly, if fleetingly, in the depths of our own being, a Creator who transcends all categories and labels. We perceive the Creator in wildness, in beauty, in art, in the surge of ideas, in communion with our fellow creatures. We meet the Creator as we would meet another person, as a center of consciousness and will and desire, yet one that overflows every limit we can imagine. This divine Being contains all lesser beings, as the ocean contains whales and fish. There is love in this enveloping presence, but also toughness; there is terrifying power as well as serenity; there is tremendous wisdom along with burning curiosity.

I believe that Creation is not finished, but rather is a fabulous experiment whose outcome not even the Creator foresees. Because the outcome is unknown, the Creator is passionately interested in its unfolding. Our universe may be one of many, each one obeying different laws, but it is the only one we humans can witness. However simple the forces that set our universe in motion, and however simple the rules that govern the evolution of those forces, the deepest impulse behind this Creation appears to be a drive toward complexity. Cosmic history reveals a gradual movement, not without occasional reverses, toward higher and higher levels of order, as matter organized itself into atoms, atoms into molecules, molecules into organisms, organisms into societies. The life on our own small planet is most likely only a sample of life in the universe. Every living species manifests the yearning of the Creator to take on form, to explore the possibilities in matter, and every species is therefore precious.

However precious it may be, everything that springs into existence eventually dissolves back to the source, making way for new gestures of being. We humans are not the endpoint of evolution, not the favorite darlings of the Creator, but only clever players in the ongoing drama. Nonetheless, we may be useful, even crucial, to the work of Creation. We have been given the distinctive and perhaps unique ability to discern the laws that govern the universe, and to express what we discover in words and images and formulas. The search for understanding and the struggle for expression are therefore the most vital of our pursuits; by comparison, the scramble for wealth, power, status, and pleasure is a mere sideshow. We matter as individuals, as societies, and as a species in proportion to what we contribute to the evolving self-awareness of the universe.

Our part in the cosmic story is to gaze back, with comprehension and joy, at the whole of Creation. Our role is to witness and celebrate the beauty of things, the elegance and order in the world, and the Ground of Being that we share with all creatures. We do this through painting and storytelling, through dancing and singing, through science and mathematics, through the raising of buildings and the launching of telescopes into space, through the shaping of poems and pots, through our never-ending talk. In however small a way, each of us helps to push outward the margins of consciousness. If any part of us survives death, it will be the ripples of new perception that we set moving in the ocean of being. All that we perceive, think, and feel is gathered up in the mind of the Creator, and the Creator, in turn, ponders and probes the universe through us. Even these sentences, even your thoughts as you read them, are filaments that flicker in the great Mind.

There, in brief, are the answers I would give now to the questions that have haunted me since my brush with death on the operating table. Of course they are always subject to change in light of new evidence and insight, but for the present they are the ones I try to live by. If elements of my vision seem familiar, it is because I have drawn images and ideas from ancient spiritual teachings, as well as from modern cosmology. In a secular age, I need make no excuse for borrowing from science. I can justify my borrowing from religion only by appealing, again, to faith: I believe that a holy power calls to us, that it provokes our wonder and reflection, that it responds to our seeking.

While the world's religions differ from one another in details of worship and doctrine, they all point more or less directly toward the same center. This congruence may be explained psychologically as a projection of human need, or biologically as an adaptation to a perilous environment, or metaphysically as a response to a potent reality that commands our attention. Since our plight as fragile creatures on a risky planet influences everything we do, there is clearly some truth in the psychological and biological explanations. But we can approach the whole truth, I am convinced, only by making the metaphysical claim. I believe the source and goal of our longing is really there, at the heart of the world.

Even if there were enough room, this would not be the place for me to explain all my reasons for believing as I do. I have sketched a few of the reasons in earlier chapters, but I would have to multiply these narratives of hope a hundredfold in order to trace the history of my search for the sacred, and I would have to stretch the boundaries of language to even hint at what I have found. I am no mystic, no seer, but an ordinary man seized by awe. I can't prove that anything I say about ultimate reality is true. I can only echo the words of a genuine mystic, Martin Buber, and confess that "nothing remains to me in the end but an appeal to the testimony of your own mysteries, my reader, which may be buried under debris but are presumably still accessible to you." My aim is not to persuade you to accept my vision, but rather to invite you to clarify your own.

At least by now you will understand why my reading of the cosmic story fills me with hope. It is reassuring to feel we are not alone in a hostile universe, but rather we are allied with a creative power which seeks us out, which strengthens and inspires us, which needs our eyes and ears and tongues. We are not puppets tugged by invisible strings, but free players in the drama of Creation. We learn the script as we go, and we also help to compose it, we and all our fellow beings. In our search for knowledge and our struggle for expression we are carrying on the Creator's work, and in that work we are aided by the Way of things. To recognize the possibility of such aid is to believe in grace. So we are justified in feeling not merely human optimism, based on a confidence in our own intelligence and skills, but cosmic optimism, based on the nature of reality.

I have not suffered from that childhood nightmare of a hammer slamming the incandescent *I* for decades, but plenty of adult nightmares have crowded in to fill the vacuum. Sometimes when I cannot sleep, or when I wake in the morning before dawn, I walk downstairs in the dark. I could turn on a light in the hall, but I don't want to disturb Ruth. So I make my way down the stairs without being able to see where I am setting my feet, yet I never doubt that the steps are there. In mild weather I often continue on outside, and if the night is moonless or overcast, I walk without hesitation over the invisible ground, trusting the earth to bear me up. To live boldly, to work effectively, we need to feel a similar confidence in the Ground of Being. We don't have to feel that it is benevolent, any more than we have to believe that the stairway or dirt is benevolent, only that it is steady, reliable, and, at least in part, knowable.

This argument for trusting in the Way of things may sound cerebral, but in my own experience the trust itself is visceral. Pascal, who knew the downward tug of despair, also knew the upwelling of hope: "In spite of . . . all our miseries, which touch us, which grip us by the throat, we have an instinct which we cannot repress and which lifts us up." If we are going to be lifted up by hope, we must feel it in our guts, through and through, the way we feel the smack of beauty or hunger or love. I cannot look on this magnificent Creation, cannot read the story of the unfolding universe, without feeling a surge of gratitude and expectation.

"We are surrounded by a rich and fertile mystery," Thoreau reminds us. "May we not probe it, pry into it, employ ourselves about it, a little? To devote your life to the discovery of the divinity in nature or to the eating of oysters, would they not be attended with very different results?" Whatever its source, Creation is a marvelous feat of generosity, an exuberant outpouring. I see that lavish gift in Ruth's face, in the wren pecking for bugs on my windowsill, in the October rain bringing down yellow leaves from the tulip tree in our front yard, in the pumpkin glowing orange on our neighbor's porch. The outpouring never ceases, but only changes form. We honor this continuing gift by our own acts of charity and compassion. We honor the Creator by cherishing every parcel of Creation, especially those living things that share the planet with us, the beetles and bison, the black-footed ferrets and black-eyed Susans.

Because we have achieved an extraordinary power to impose our will upon the earth, we bear a solemn obligation to conserve the earth's bounty, for all life. This means we should defend the air and water and soil from pollution and exploitation. It means that we should protect other species and preserve the habitats on which they rely. For our own species, it means we should bring into the world only those children for whom we can provide adequate care, and then we should provide that care lovingly and generously. Since we carry on the work of Creation through acts of inquiry and imagination, we should safeguard the freedom of thought and expression. Since every single one of us may contribute to the growth of consciousness, we should work to guarantee every human being the chance to develop his or her potential.

The price of hope, in other words, is responsibility. In exchange for the gift of purpose, in exchange for grace, we are called to account for our lives. I am aware that anyone who looks for divinity in nature may be dismissed as a wishful thinker. I may well be the dupe of my own craving for direction. And yet it seems to me far more wishful to believe that the universe requires nothing of us, that we need be guided only by our appetites, whether for oysters or for some other delicacies, than to believe that there is a sacred authority to which we are answerable. My reading of the cosmic story implies that we *are* answerable, to a high and rigorous standard enforced by an ultimate power, and that in our best moments we may answer well.

FOURTEEN

MOUNTAIN
MUSIC IV

ON A SULTRY AUGUST AFTERNOON in the Smoky Mountains, a year after our quarrel in the Rockies, Jesse and I fell to talking about God. It was Jesse who brought up this grandest of all subjects, and he did most of the talking, because we were climbing a steep trail with loaded packs and he was the only one with a supply of breath.

"I remember when I was little," he said, "and it dawned on me one day that everything alive was filled with God."

"You must have been eight," I said, huffing. "Maybe nine."

"And then I realized that the grass was alive, and the dirt was alive, and suddenly I was afraid of setting my foot down because I'd be walking on God. I remember we were playing baseball in Bryan Park."

"You were chasing a fly ball. Then you just stopped."

"I stood there in the outfield, calling you. I was so scared."

"Sprained ankle, I figured. Or a bee sting."

"You carried me all the way home."

"And you were a load, let me tell you." I grunted, took a few more panting steps, then halted. "You must have weighed as much as this pack."

Jesse turned on me those gleaming brown eyes that have always made me think of Ruth. "Want a break?" he asked.

"Good idea." I wiped a forearm across my slick face. "It's not that I'm tired. I just don't want to wear you out on the first day."

We rested on the trunk of a fallen hemlock, sharing a bottle of water and a handful of raisins. Butterflies lilted past us, heading up the slope, hundreds of them in dozens of colors, feeding on the gangly flowers that grew in the rare openings along the trail. The valley of the Little Tennessee River, where we had parked the car, lay a few miles behind us, and the campsite we were aiming for lay a few miles farther on. Rain had followed us all the way south from Indiana on our drive that morning, and here in the mountains, a ranger told us, it had been raining for most of a week. The gray sky threatened more rain, but so far it was holding back. Creeks rushed down the slope on both sides of the trail, enveloping us in murmurs and mist. I drew in lungfuls of dank air.

"It really freaked me out," Jesse said, "to realize that God was in the grass, in the dirt, in bugs on the sidewalk and in the mashed potatoes on my plate. Either God was everywhere, or he was nowhere. He couldn't just be inside a church or a book. He couldn't be trapped just inside human beings, or even just on earth."

"What do you think about all of that now?" I asked.

"Obviously I got over the fear of walking." Jesse leaned forward on the log and glanced down at his mud-caked boots, which had carried him around Europe earlier in the summer, and on previous treks through mountains, gorges, creeks, and forests in half a dozen states. "And I lost my confidence in talking about God," he added. What he had not lost, he went on to say, was his feeling that a great and mysterious power works through all things; he still wondered how we might contact that power and where it might be leading us.

On this journey, by mutual consent, Jesse was leading us. The trip had been his idea, a last chance to stretch his legs and sleep on dirt before he started college. I'd asked if he wanted to bring along a couple of his hiking buddies, but he insisted that the two of us go alone. "I feel like I haven't really talked with you in months," he said. He planned the meals, packed the gear, studied the maps. When I offered to help, he shrugged his big shoulders and answered, "No problem. I've got it under control." He was familiar with the Smokies, had even hiked this mountain loop twice before with friends. In every way except age, Jesse was the veteran here and I was the tenderfoot. Sensing his need to play the leader, I honored this reversal of roles.

"You figure we'll reach the campsite before dark?" I asked him.

"For sure. The trail levels out pretty soon, runs through a stretch of pines, crosses the creek three or four times. Then we'll be there. You ready to go for it?"

"Ready as I'll ever be."

At the rapid swinging pace that suited his long legs he set out up the trail, which zigzagged along switchbacks through stands of ash and oak, sassafras and maple, hemlock and tulip poplar. The temperature fell as we climbed. Sure enough, the muddy track soon leveled out, then ran on through a plantation of pines. But I lost my breath anyway, humping along under the weight of my pack. So I mainly listened while Jesse told me that he wondered if humans might be poised to break through into a new level of consciousness. He wondered if maybe that's what lay behind all our troubles. Maybe God was urging us toward a new vision of our place in the world, a vision more tender and peaceful and spiritual.

In his words I could hear echoes of the Buddha and Jesus and mystics the world over. But I didn't say so, not wanting to rub the freshness from his insight.

"We need to be more loving," he said. "It's like our hearts need to catch up with our brains and hands." He trudged on a few paces in silence, then stopped, as abruptly as on that long ago day in the park when he had stood paralyzed in the grass by the fear of treading on God. He swung around to face me. "Do you believe we can change? That we're not stuck in this dead-end way of thinking?"

The intensity in his face and voice demanded the truth. So I considered carefully before answering. "Yes I do."

Jesse gazed at me for a moment, no longer as a boy studying his father but as one man testing another. Then relief spread through him visibly, softening his face, relaxing his body. "That makes two of us."

"Enough to start a movement," I suggested.

"Or join one."

"You mean other people?"

"I mean other people," he said. "And whatever else may be heading in the right direction."

With about an hour of daylight left, we reached our campsite in a cove at the junction of three creeks. As in the Rockies a year before, so here in the Smokies, every stream was swollen, and the purr of tumbling water rubbed over us. We laid out our gear on a poncho and pitched our tent on the damp ground. The rain still held off, yet everything was already soaked, including the dead branches we gathered for a fire. The dampness must have been perennial, because the trees were clad in moss and lichens, not only down among the roots but well above our heads. Ferns curled up everywhere from rotting logs the color of bricks, mushrooms thrust pale thumbs up through matted leaves, and rhododendrons arched over the creeks. In the gathering darkness, tree frogs began to call, soon loudly enough to rival the racket of hustling water.

In spite of the dampness, I managed to get a fire started, and to keep it going with a steady flame. Jesse cooked burritos on our tiny gas stove, frying hamburger and stirring in peppers and onions and seasoning. He insisted on doing all the cooking, not only for this meal but for the whole trip, so I volunteered to wash dishes. This amused him, because he and his buddies never bothered with cleaning up, figuring that grease and grot were essential to the woods experience. After we ate, Jesse was even more amused that I stripped off all my sweaty clothes and waded into the froth of a creek to bathe. He kidded me about going soft from my indoor life. I kidded him in turn about how black bears are drawn to the stink of unbathed hikers. The truth was that I cared less about getting clean than about lying naked in the rush of water. The creek was cold and I shivered when I stood up dripping in the mountain air.

It felt good to sit beside the fire while the gray sky turned black. Jesse read *The Moor's Last Sigh*, by Salman Rushdie, and I wrote in my notebook, both of us tilting our pages to catch the flickering light. I kept glancing at him, his face so absorbed, the gingery beard glinting on his jaw, the shoulder-length blond hair drawn back in a pony-tail, the fathomless brown eyes. On our drive from Indiana, he had told me that the summer of tramping in Europe had restored his love of reading. He'd lost his way in high school, he said, lost any clear sense of why he was getting those straight A's. During his travels that summer, bumping into other students, sleeping on borrowed floors, riding all-night trains to ancient cities that were brand-new to him, slouching through museums, reading novels in sidewalk cafes, he'd rediscovered the point of learning. And what is that? I asked. "It's fun," he answered. "It enlarges your life, and it prepares you to do some good in the world."

Reading now by firelight, Jesse looked up from his book every once in a while to recall something about those weeks in Europe.

"I'd meet strangers," he said at one point, "maybe in a youth hostel or train station, or crossing a street, and they'd stare at me as though they knew me somehow. We'd find a language we could talk—English, usually, or maybe French, or some fractured Spanish—and I would ask a few questions. And before I knew it, people I'd never seen before were telling me their life stories, and it was like I'd run into lost brothers or sisters." Now he figured that everyone he met had something to teach him, if only about what to avoid on his path through life.

A while later, Jesse asked me what I was scribbling in my notebook.

"What happened today, more or less," I answered.

"For your book on hope?"

"Some of it may wind up there."

"Including what I say?"

"Could be. Do you mind?"

He pondered that a spell, rubbing the bristle on his chin. Sap sizzled in the coals. Finally he said, "It's okay, so long as I don't come off as a fool kid."

"You're the hero," I told him. "One of the heroes, anyway."

He looked at me hard to make sure I wasn't teasing. "Must be a strange book."

Light rain eventually drove us into the tent, where we lay shoulder to shoulder, with our jeans rolled up under our heads for pillows. Within minutes Jesse was asleep. Too tired for sleep, I lay there listening. No wind, no creak of limbs, no grumble of engines, only water song and frog song and our entwined breaths.

Jesse had changed a great deal, and so had I, in the year since we'd quarreled in Big Thompson Canyon and rafted down the river and turned back in the face of lightning over Thunder Lake. I'd spent the year trying to see the world through his eyes, through Eva's eyes, through the eyes of my students, while working on this book. Whatever my words might eventually mean to these young people, the effort to speak of hope had renewed my own courage. Meanwhile Jesse finished high school, decided to stay in our hometown for college, grieved over the death of his best friend's father, saw other friends succumb to dope or drink or depression, and then for six weeks he'd backpacked around Europe, time enough for him to savor his newfound independence, miss his family, and take on responsibility for his life.

I didn't understand all of the changes, in him or in me, but on the whole they seemed to me blessings. We'd become friends once more. There was an ease in our talk and work together that I had not felt with him for half a dozen years. I could groan over the country music he played on the car radio as we drove south, and instead of taking offense he would laugh. And he could tell me to chill out when I worried aloud about hillsides of pines in the Smokies turning brown, and I felt no urge to lecture him about acid rain. I still could not turn off my fathering mind, but I could turn down the volume, quiet the fretful voice, and enjoy the company of my grown son, without worrying constantly, as I had the year before, that at any moment our voices might begin clashing like swords.

We woke inside a cloud. Trees loomed around us like ghostly columns, their upper branches veiled in white. The creeks purred on, invisible, but the frogs had hushed.

"Where'd everything go?" Jesse muttered, then rolled over in his sleeping bag.

I lay there remembering a park sign we had come across the day before, which explained that three-quarters of the haze in the air that gave these mountains their name now comes from pollution, and only one-quarter from gases released by decaying matter. There was plenty of matter for decay in these old woods, in the leaf duff and downed logs and spongy soil.

I pulled on cold jeans and crawled from the tent and walked on stiff legs to filter drinking water from the nearest creek. Mist rode the current, wafting and spinning under the boughs of rhododendrons, their leaves dangling like green donkey's ears. Hearing a twig crack behind me, I turned, thinking it was Jesse, but it was a deer, coming to drink at the creek maybe ten paces from where I squatted. It looked to be a yearling doe, slender and neat. She stood with her forefeet close together and bent her muzzle to the water and the muscles in her neck rippled as she swallowed. Water had never seemed so good to me as it did while I watched her drink. Then I did hear Jesse, the tramp of his boots coming my way, and in the same instant the deer jerked her head up, pricked up her ears, spun around in one convulsive motion with white tail raised and bounded off noisily into the fog.

"Did you see the deer?" Jesse asked wonderingly as he drew close to me.

"Wasn't she a beauty?"

"For a second there I thought maybe it was a bear."

Jesse took over from me, pumping water through the filter into our plastic bottles, and as he worked he told about sighting bears on his previous trips into the Smokies. Once he and his two partners had swung around a bend in the trail, and there sat a mother and her cub, feeding on blackberries, sleek fur gleaming in the noonday sun. Jesse knew better than to crowd a cub, so he and his buddies just stood there while the bears ate with long red tongues and much blinking of shiny black eyes. It seemed the bears would never tire of berries, so eventually Jesse and his buddies circled out through the woods and rejoined the trail at a safe distance beyond.

"I'm dressed for them," he said, pointing at his chest.

He wore a clean white T-shirt from a Grateful Dead concert. The words on the front posed a question—WHAT DO YOU DO IF YOU MEET A BEAR IN THE WOOD?—and the back offered an answer: PLAY DEAD. Despite the morning chill, his thick legs jutted out bare from cut-off jeans.

"Aren't you cold?" I asked.

"Not so long as I keep moving."

We tightened the caps on our water bottles. Every time I drank from mine that day I would think of the deer, and of how generous the world is to satisfy our thirst.

After a breakfast of omelets with green peppers, we broke camp and shouldered the packs and made our way uphill through cloud. The trees might have stopped ten feet above our heads, for all we could see of their branches, and only their bark and the nuts and acorns underfoot identified them as mostly oak and hickory. The trail was littered with broken stone, and the root-balls from fallen trees exposed the shattered bedrock that lay everywhere beneath thin soil, reminders that these were old, snaggle-toothed mountains, far older than the Rockies, and they had been eroding for three hundred million years.

Although it was August, prime vacation season in the Smokies, we had met no one on our hike the day before, and this day we met only a father and his two young daughters clumping down-hill looking bedraggled. Jesse and I stepped back to let them pass. The girls' hair frizzed out beneath baseball caps and they peered up at us with glum expressions. The father paused long enough to say they had planned to stay longer, but every stitch of clothing they had with them was soaked through, and no prospect of dry-ing out any time soon, so they were packing it in.

At midmorning we came to a grassy clearing that gave us a view of the sky, what there was of it, and we could see a hint of sun to the east like a single dim headlight on an idle train. By noon, when we stopped for lunch on the open crest of a mountain, the light had chugged on overhead but had grown no brighter, and the sky glowed a pale indigo. We shucked off our packs and hunched down on our spread-out ponchos and ate peanut butter sandwiches, breathing vapor. A few butterflies lolled past, their colors washed out, and they fed on thistles bleached white by cloud. We could see mist easing by on a wind too subtle for hear-ing. Even these few glimpses of the ghostly world came to us only because this mountain top was bare of trees, one of those open-ings in the Smokies known as balds. What originally kept the for-est back, whether grazing long ago by deer and elk and even bi-son, or maybe fires lit by lightning or Cherokees, no one knows, but these openings show up on the earliest surveys of the moun-tains, from the 1820s, and now the Park Service works to keep them clear. Jesse had wanted to show me the panorama visible from this peak on a clear day, but on this day of swirling whiteness he could only describe for me what I might have seen.

"Sounds beautiful," I said when he had finished.

"It is," he agreed. "Way beyond words."

I washed down the last of my sandwich with some of the creek water I had shared with the deer, and then I left Jesse reading his novel while I went out to hunt for blueberries. After only a dozen paces I looked back and could barely make out his dark silhouette in the cottony air. Not wanting to lose sight of him, I traced out a slow circle with Jesse at the center. Moist grass lapped against my legs, and seedling pines, and cardinal flowers shimmering a dull red, until I came to a patch of low bushes covered with berries that looked in this vaporous air like silver beads. Even blanched of color they were blueberries, all right, as my tongue quickly told me. I picked less by sight than by touch, tilted a handful into my mouth, and savored the burst of tangy sweetness. I ate a second handful and a third, understanding why bears would not quit eating so long as the flavor stayed fresh. Thought of bears made me keep glancing up as I picked, on the lookout for a burly shape heaving toward me through the mist.

The fourth handful I carried back to Jesse, who sat as I had left him, with the book balanced on his lifted knees. He accepted the blueberries with thanks and began popping them into his mouth a few at a time, never taking his eyes from the page. Again I circled away from him, this time with our two drinking cups, and when I returned both cups were heaped with berries.

"You leave any for the poor bears?" Jesse asked.

"A few," I assured him.

We sat there among the drifting clouds munching the tart berries, and I could not tell whether the ones I ate or the ones my son ate gave me more pleasure.

The campsite for our second night was a favorite of Jesse's from previous trips, on a flat ridgetop among old trees growing wide apart. Before setting up he led me around the place eagerly, as if it were a haunt of his childhood, showing me a huge log the color of bone, where he liked to stretch out, a heap of windblown gray birches where he always gathered firewood, a spring oozing over mossy ledges into a fern-fringed pool where he drew his water, a clearing where he watched the stars.

We would see no stars that night, nor much of anything else during the day, for the dense cloud shut off vision at a distance of fifty feet or so. Jesse and I worked along as though wrapped in fleece. Practiced at making camp, we hardly spoke as we pitched the shivering blue tent upwind from the stone ring of the fire pit, strung a line to hang out our wet socks and shirts in air as damp as they were, then rigged my poncho among four scrawny trees to make an awning against the rain that was sure to come. While Jesse cobbled together a rough bench by lashing dead limbs together, I ranged about gathering firewood. Every snag looming in the mist could have been a crouching animal. Once as I straightened up with a handful of sticks I nearly cried out, certain I had seen a bear. I bit my lip, realizing it was only a stump, but my heart took a long while in settling down.

The rain came on before I had started the fire, at first only a thickening of the mist and then a drizzle, as if the clouds we had been breathing all day had suddenly congealed. Jesse and I sat on his rough bench under the awning while rain pattered down, both of us chilled to the bone. He stared out at the circle of blackened stones. "I sure was looking forward to that fire," he muttered.

"We'll have us a fire," I told him.

"How? In the rain?"

"Let me think here a minute." We had brought no paper along except for the map and Jesse's novel and my notebook, and we would shiver all night before sacrificing any of them. Wondering what else we could use for tinder, I remembered a trick my father had taught me. "You ever see any grapevines around here?"

Jesse shut his eyes, thinking, then pointed along the ridge. "I believe there's a tangle just off the path to the spring."

"Go see if you can find them, and strip off a wad of the loose bark, and zip it in your driest pocket and bring it back here."

He trudged away through the fine rain and the blue of his jacket soon disappeared among the dark pillars of the trees. Under the makeshift awning I took out my knife and began whittling a stick, letting the curls of wood fall into our frying pan. By the time Jesse returned with a double handful of grapevine bark, I had filled the pan with shavings. I took the stringy bark and rubbed it back and forth between my palms to shred it, and then I added the bark to my pile of shavings.

"Now I need you to hold my jacket over me while I lay the fire," I told him, slipping my arms from the sleeves.

"Use mine," he offered.

"I've been wet before."

I handed him the jacket. Bending over to protect the pan full of tinder from the rain, I stepped out beyond the edge of the awning to kneel over the fire pit. Jesse followed and leaned above me, spreading the jacket like a single flimsy wing to shelter me. I laid the shredded bark in the cinders left by other campers and covered it with the shavings and tilted over them a pyramid of twigs and sticks and cut branches as long and thick as my forearm. Then I drew the match case from my shirt pocket, unscrewed the lid, pulled out a wooden match, struck it along the sandpapery side of the case, and held the flame cupped in my hand. Before I could reach the tinder, the match guttered out, and so did a second one and a third.

"This isn't going to work," Jesse predicted.

"Don't give up yet," I answered, striking a fourth match.

A gust of wind blew out this one, and the next. Rain rattled the jacket over my head and mist blew around me.

"We'll get by," Jesse said.

"We'll get by better with a fire."

I struck another match, encircled it with my palm, reached through a gap in the pyramid of glistening wood and pressed the flame into the nest of bark and shavings. The flame wavered, licking up into the cone of twigs, but would spread no farther without more air. I tilted my face and bent down until my cheek nearly grazed the blackened stones and blew gently. A few twigs caught, but they glowed only so long as I kept puffing at them. When I stopped for a breath the flame sank down.

"We need something to fan it with," I said.

"All right," Jesse answered, "but as soon as I move the rain's going to put it out."

"Just be quick. I'll keep it covered."

I stooped over the faltering fire with my eyes closed against the smoke. Steam hissed from the wet wood and rain drummed on my back. After a few moments of rummaging about under the awning, Jesse returned and nudged me aside. I backed out of the smoke and squinted up to see him waving at the fire with his thick novel encased in a plastic bag. Flames quickly ran up the twigs and wound among the sticks. I laid on a few more branches from our pile.

"Don't smother it," he said.

I started to ask him whose fire he thought this was, anyway, but I held back, remembering that we were on his ground, following his trail, and that I had accepted him as the leader on this journey. He'd earned the right, as a veteran in these mountains and as a boy grown up into his man's body.

I stepped back under the awning. "Let me know when you want me to fan for a while."

By the time he offered me a turn the flames were leaping and there was no need for any more fanning. Shivering, we pulled on dry clothes and sat again on the bench with shoulders touching and stared at the flames until our shivers died down. Smoke mixed with steam and rain to cloud the air. The last remnants of light drained from the sky. Soon there was nothing to see but the fire seething and sparks flying up.

"You hungry yet?" Jesse asked.

"I could eat anything that won't eat me," I answered.

He cooked, I fed the fire. We ate slowly, talking of the day, and then I washed up. Rain dripped from the edges of our lean-to, but the heat from the fire enfolded us against the evening chill. I took out the notebook and wrote my own version of the day in a crooked scrawl. Jesse pulled back his lank hair and bound it in place with an elastic band stretched across his forehead. He propped a small flashlight over his right ear and tucked the butt of it up under the elastic band, then he switched on the light and tilted it down so that it shone on the pages of his book.

"You look like a miner," I said.

When he glanced at me, the flashlight dazzled my eyes. "What's that?"

"Never mind. I'm just talking."

"You never run short of words," he observed with a smile, then returned to his reading.

No, I never run short of words, but finding the right ones and yoking them together into sentences that ring true and laying out sentences page after page into a necessary order is always a struggle. To say the simplest thing may baffle me. No piling on of words can ever fully tell how much I love my son, my daughter, my wife, how much I honor my students, how much I exult in this world we briefly share.

"Good fire we built," Jesse said after a while. He switched off the flashlight, pulled it from his headband, and sat staring into the flames. "Even the rain won't put it out."

"Not unless it rains a lot harder," I said.

The two of us watched embers fade and glow as the wind breathed on them. The smell of wet ashes mixed with the smell of burning sap. Rain rattled on the stretched skin of my poncho overhead and hissed as it struck the coals. The sound set me humming.

"You like these mountains?" Jesse asked.

"I do."

"I don't know why, but the mountains make me believe we can change." His dark eyes mirrored the fire. "Maybe not everybody. But at least enough people to start us in a new direction."

"Keep on believing that," I told him, "and you're halfway there."

The fire kept stilling our tongues. Flames whipped from the tops of burning sticks like orange flags. Sparks rose into the dark and dwindled to the size of stars and winked out, and new sparks followed. An old patched-together prayer rose in me:

> My God, my God, my holy one, my love,
> May I be open and balanced and peaceful.

I breathed in with the first line, breathed out with the second, and that breathing seemed to me the whole of the story we the living have to tell.

LIVING IN HOPE

MORE THAN A YEAR HAS GONE BY since Jesse and I built a fire in the rain, but the notebook I carried on that mountain journey still smells of wood smoke. More than two years have passed since we quarreled in the Rockies, but his words about the need for hope still ring in my head as if he had just quit speaking. "You've got me seeing nothing but darkness," he tells me, his voice cracking with pain. "I have to believe there's a way we can get out of this mess. Otherwise what's the point? Why study, why work, why do anything if it's all going to hell?"

I cannot scour from my vision the darkness that troubles my son, because I have witnessed too much suffering and waste, I know too much about what humans are doing to one another and to the planet. I cannot answer Jesse's questions about hope, or Eva's, or those of my students, by pretending that I see no reasons for despair. Anyone who pays attention to the state of the world knows that we are in trouble. Anyone who looks honestly at the human prospect realizes that we face enormous challenges: population growth, environmental degradation, extinction of species, ethnic and racial strife, doomsday weapons, epidemic disease, drugs, poverty, hunger, and crime, to mention only a few. These stark realities press on my mind as I write. What I have been saying in this book is that they are not the only realities, nor the most powerful or durable ones. I see light shining in the darkness. I live in hope.

"What's the good of grieving if you can't change anything?" Jesse demanded of me during our quarrel in the Rocky Mountains. A year later, amidst the rushing of streams in the Smokies, he put the question more calmly but no less intently: "Do you believe we can change? That we're not stuck in this dead-end way of thinking?"

I answered yes that day; I am answering yes now. My search for hope has convinced me that we *can* change our ways of seeing and thinking and living. We can begin living responsibly and alertly right where we are, right now, no matter how troubled we may be about the human prospect. If we set out to solve the world's problems, we are likely to feel overwhelmed. On the other hand, if we set out to act on our deepest concerns and convictions we may do some good. We can begin making changes in our own lives without waiting for such changes to become popular, without knowing whether they will have any large-scale effect, but merely because we believe they are right.

For my part, I believe that all but the poorest of us could choose to lead materially simpler lives, and thereby do less harm and reap more joy. We could learn to be guided by what we need rather than by what the hucksters urge us to want. We could ignore fashion and hype, and look for true quality—in products, services, art, and people. We could work toward a more just distribution of wealth, within our own country and among nations. We could re-imagine ourselves as conservers rather than consumers—conservers of land and air and water and all the earth's bounty, conservers of human achievements from the past and human potential for the future, conservers of beauty and wildness.

If we are determined to live in hope, we could make a more serious commitment to sustaining our families, recognizing that, in spite all their flaws, they are the best means we have for nurturing children and fostering love. We could re-imagine ourselves as inhabitants rather than tourists, cultivating a stronger sense of place, learning about the land, its natural and human history, and the needs of our communities. We could decide to stay put, in our houses and neighborhoods, unless we have compelling reasons to move. We could think hard before we jump in a car or an airplane and zoom off, making sure each trip is worth what it costs the earth. Instead of rushing about, we could slow down, center down, and open ourselves to the five rivers of the senses.

We could learn to satisfy more of our own needs ourselves, with help from families and neighbors and friends. When we buy goods and services, we could give more of our business to local farmers, artists, craftspeople, skilled workers, merchants and manufacturers, and to locally owned enterprises, since people who share a place with us are more likely to care for it than strangers are. We could accept more graciously our responsibilities as citizens, informing ourselves about public matters, taking our turn at public service, honoring the necessity of government and making sure that our representatives govern well. In the inevitable clash of private interests, we could speak up for the common good.

As we transform our own lives, we join with others who are making a kindred effort, and thus our work will be multiplied a thousandfold across the country and a millionfold around the earth. Whether all such efforts, added together, will be enough to avert disaster and bring about a just and enduring way of life, no one can say. In order to live in hope we needn't believe that everything will turn out well. We need only believe that we are on the right path.

What endures? What lifts our hearts? What do we possess in abundance? For most of our history, we newcomers to America have imagined that animals, trees, water, soil, and clean air are inexhaustible, when they are in fact limited and vulnerable. We have considered peace and prosperity and civil order to be our birthright, when they are in fact hard won and easily lost. Our truly abundant resources are mostly intangible, difficult to describe and impossible to measure, and among them are love, beauty, skill, compassion, community, fidelity, simplicity, and wildness. Through cruelty or carelessness we can destroy the conditions that nurture these powers, but the powers themselves are not used up in our experience of them.

To keep up my courage for the journey, I carry tokens of these healing and nourishing powers in my medicine bundle of words: a leaping dog, a necklace of shell and bone, the splash of water over stone, a screech owl calling through storm, a comet returning, a galaxy snared on a computer screen, apple trees bearing fruit near a stream in the desert, a man teaching homeless children how to make music, the image of a woman cupping her breasts, a baby staring, a welder making sure a railing stands plumb and true, my mother laboring up the steps on her reconstructed knee with an armful of flowers, Eva's face shining through her bridal veil, Jesse's dark eyes lit by starlight, the murmur of Ruth's heart.

I write these last paragraphs on the first day of a new year. Thin snow covers our patch of Indiana and the day has dawned clear. With early sunlight streaming in the windows, Ruth and I take down the Christmas decorations, wrap the handmade ornaments in tissue paper, loop the colored lights into bundles, and store everything away in the attic. I carry the tree out the back door and across the yard, leaving a trail of needles the whole way, and lay it behind the wood pile to provide shelter for the birds. Thinking of birds, I refill the feeders. No sooner have I finished pouring seeds and backed away than a nuthatch swoops down, claims a beakful, and flies off. Next come chickadee, blue jay, titmouse, cardinal, each one quick and bright, a spark from the one great fire.

The birds in turn make me think of Eva, who has just begun research for her doctoral dissertation on how birds learn. She wants to know how much of what birds do is passed down through their genes, automatic as the color of feather or eye, and how much is learned from adults of their own kind. She and Matt have been married now for six months, and they're still figuring out what they both like to eat. After lunch she'll be coming over to discuss recipes with Ruth. My mother will also be coming over this afternoon, to go through some old family photographs and help me put names to faces. We hope to see Jesse today as well, but we can never be sure when he'll turn up. He's a sophomore now, studying history and economics, and living this year with four other guys in a house about a mile west of us. He still bristles when I challenge him, but now that he lives on his own I have fewer occasions to challenge him.

Jesse has come to mind this New Year's morning as I split lengths of firewood into kindling, for I keep remembering the day when he and I and Matt and Don Allen, two pairs of fathers and sons, cut up that drift log on the bank of Clear Creek. Today each blow of the axe releases the secret, musty smell of red oak, like the fragrance of an old bouquet. The air is so mild that the snow melts rapidly, and as I tramp between woodpile and back porch with armloads of kindling the ground squishes beneath my boots.

Every half hour or so throughout the morning I interrupt whatever else I'm doing to line up another plastic jug beneath a downspout, where I'm catching snowmelt from the roof to use in watering our house plants. When I've gathered five gallons Ruth signals to me through the front porch window, with a laugh I can see but not hear, that I needn't fill any more jugs.

Still wearing the laugh on her face, she opens the door and hands me a brown envelope. "Here," she says, "if you're looking for excuses to stay outside, why don't you plant the jack-in-the-pulpits?"

"Isn't it too cold?" I ask.

"The seeds need the cold now so they can recognize spring when it comes."

I put the envelope in my back pocket, and with a hoe I clear a spot in the snow near the base of our tulip tree in the front yard. As I'm scraping aside the mat of leaves, Jesse comes jogging up in shorts and sweatshirt, leading his housemate's new puppy, a golden retriever named Miles. The puppy's tongue is hanging out and in the sunshine his fur gleams with a color close to that of Jesse's wet blond hair. Man and dog are both panting.

"What a day to start the year!" Jesse exclaims.

"Isn't it amazing?" I reply.

Jesse hunkers down to pat the puppy, who laps at his face. "Miles and I ran all over the neighborhood. Didn't we, little guy? We've been out so long it must be getting close to lunchtime."

"Pretty soon," I agree. "You know anybody who might want to stay and eat?"

"Well, I could be persuaded. And Miles could use a drink."

"Go get cleaned up, then, and tell Mom I'll be along in two shakes."

"Are Eva and Matt coming over?"

"Yes. And so is Mimi."

"Cool. A regular family occasion." Jesse bounds onto the porch with the puppy at his heels and the two disappear inside.

I return to my little clearing in the snow, and with the hoe I loosen the black soil and scatter the bright red seeds of jack-in-the-pulpit. As I'm covering the seeds with dirt and leaves and tamping them down with my boots, I do not merely remember, I *feel* the root meaning of hope: to leap up in expectation.

"Memory grips the past," as my friend wrote to me, "and hope grips the future." I think of the scarlet seeds quietly burning against the cold black dirt, waiting for spring. I think of my children, and of the children they may have one day, and of those children's children, on and on, like ridge upon ridge of mountains stretching out before me as far as I can see. I think of my students hard at work learning what our clever species has already discovered, and adding their own new knowledge to the store. I imagine the host of ancestors, human and nonhuman, whose lives and labors have made this moment possible for those of us who breathe. I draw a breath, savor it, and bless them all.

Notes

EPIGRAPHS

vii   The first epigraph is a saying attributed to Confucius
        by Chuang Tzu, as quoted in Thomas Merton's *The
        Way of Chuang Tzu* (New York: New Directions, 1965),
        p. 53; the second comes from Simone Weil, *Waiting for
        God*, trans. Emma Caufurd (New York: Harper & Row,
        1973), p. 128; and the last from Alexis de Tocqueville,
        Democracy in America, ed. Richard D. Heffner (New
        York: New American Library, 1956), p. 38.

WHERE THE SEARCH BEGINS

2   Aldo Leopold, *A Sand County Almanac* (New York:
        Ballantine, 1970), p. 197.

LEAPING UP IN EXPECTATION

18   Dickinson's lines on hope appear in poem #254 in *The
        Poems of Emily Dickinson*, vol. 1, ed. Thomas H. John-
        son (Cambridge, Massachusetts: Harvard University
        Press, 1955), p. 182.

19   Job 7:3–6 (Revised Standard Version).

19   John M. Synge, *The Aran Islands* (Marlboro, Vermont:
        Marlboro Press, 1989; first published 1907), p. 83. The
        spelling of "drownded" is Synge's.

20–21   Viktor M. Frankl, *Man's Search for Meaning*, 4th ed.
        (Boston: Beacon Press, 1992), p. 82.

22   The friend who wrote the postcard about hope is Tony
        Stoneburner, of Granville, Ohio, retired professor

of English from Denison University and Methodist minister.

24   The two passages from Hebrews appear in chapter 11:1–3 and 13–16 (RSV).

24–25   I quote Paul from 1 Corinthians 13:13 and Colossians 1:3–5 (RSV).

25   Voltaire and Nietzsche are quoted in *A New Dictionary of Quotations on Historical Principles from Ancient and Modern Sources*, ed. H. L. Mencken (New York: Knopf, 1942), p. 549. I found Mencken's own comment in *Webster's New World Dictionary of Quotable Definitions*, 2nd ed., ed. Eugene E. Brussell (Englewood Cliffs, New Jersey: Prentice-Hall, 1988), p. 265.

25   Amos 5:24 (RSV).

26   Isaiah 2:4 (RSV).

26   The otherworldly remark of Jesus appears in John 8:23 (RSV).

26–27   Vaclav Havel's words come from *Disturbing the Peace: A Conversation with Karel Hvizdala* (New York: Knopf, 1990), p. 181.

WILDNESS

29   Thoreau's comment on the doleful music of screech owls appears in the "Sounds" chapter of *Walden*. I quote here from the edition edited by J. Lyndon Shanley (Princeton, New Jersey: Princeton University Press, 1973), pp. 124–25.

29   Pliny is quoted in Edward Howe Forbush and John Bichard May, *A Natural History of American Birds of Eastern and Central North America* (New York: Bramhall House, 1955), p. 261.

30   John James Audubon's anecdote appears in *The Original Water-Color Portraits for the Birds of America* (New York: American Heritage, 1966), plate 26.

35   Gerard Manley Hopkins, "God's Grandeur," in *Selected Poems*, ed. James Reeves (London: Heinemann, 1953), p. 18.

37   I learned about ecological restoration efforts in Chicago and elsewhere from William K. Stevens, *Miracle Under the Oaks: The Revival of Nature in America* (New York: Pocket, 1995).

37   Stephanie Mills, *In Service of the Wild: Restoring and Reinhabiting Damaged Land* (Boston: Beacon Press, 1995), p. 140.

37–38   The effects of the Conservation Reserve Program are reported by William K. Stevens in "U.S. Effort to Return Farm Land to Natural State Wins Praise," *New York Times*, 10 January 1995, p. B7.

38   The figures for threatened species come from Les Line, "1,096 Mammal and 1,108 Bird Species Threatened," *New York Times*, 8 October 1996, p. B6.

39   *H. D. Thoreau: A Writer's Journal*, ed. Laurence Stapleton (New York: Dover, 1960), p. 134.

39   John Muir, *My First Summer in the Sierra* (New York: Penguin, 1987; first published 1911), pp. 242–43.

39   Brother Lawrence, *The Practice of the Presence of God* (Oxford, England: Oneworld, 1993), p. 3.

40   The recent discoveries from the Hubble Space Telescope are reported by John Noble Wilford in "Suddenly, Universe Gains 40 Billion More Galaxies," *New York Times*, 16 January 1996, pp. A1, B10.

BODY BRIGHT

44   Mary Oliver, "The Plum Trees," *American Primitive* (Boston: Little, Brown, 1983), p. 84.

46   Blake's celebration of the nakedness of woman appears in "The Marriage of Heaven and Hell," plate 8 (1790–93). I quote *Blake's Poetry and Designs*, ed. Mary

Lynn Johnson and John E. Grant (New York: Norton, 1979), p. 89.

51 Carl Jung, *Modern Man in Search of a Soul* (New York: Harcourt Brace, 1933), pp. 215, 217.

51 Frankl, *Man's Search for Meaning*, p. 84.

52 Norman Cousins, *Head First: The Biology of Hope* (New York: Dutton, 1989), pp. 2–3.

53 I quote Blake again from "The Marriage of Heaven and Hell," this time from plate 4. See Johnson and Grant, ed., *Blake's Poetry and Designs*, p. 87.

53–54 D. H. Lawrence, "New Mexico," *Phoenix* (London: Heinemann, 1936), pp.146–47.

54 Mary Oliver, "Morning Poem," *Dream Work* (New York: Atlantic Monthly, 1986), p. 7.

56 Gary Snyder, *A Place in Space: Ethics, Aesthetics, and Watersheds* (Washington, D.C.: Counterpoint, 1995), p. 142.

56 Blake's famous lines about the doors of perception appear in plate 14 of "The Marriage of Heaven and Hell." See Johnson and Grant, ed., *Blake's Poetry and Designs*, p. 93.

56–57 The first passage by Thoreau comes from Stapleton, ed., *H. D. Thoreau: A Writer's Journal*, p. 175, and the second from H. Daniel Peck, ed., *A Year in Thoreau's Journal: 1851* (New York: Penguin, 1993), p. 325.

57 Adrienne Rich, "Contradictions: Tracking Poems," *Your Native Land, Your Life* (New York: Norton, 1986), p. 100.

FAMILY

64 I borrowed Thich Nhat Hanh's meditation from *Living Buddha, Living Christ* (New York: Putnam, 1995), p. 16.

68 Jared Diamond reports on evidence for care of the elderly among early humans, and speculates on the im-

portance of elders for the survival of tribes, in *The Third Chimpanzee: The Evolution and Future of the Human Animal* (New York: Harper Perennial, 1993), especially pp. 44, 122–36.

69 Gary Snyder, *The Real Work: Interviews & Talks, 1964–79*, ed. William Scott McLean (New York: New Directions, 1980), p. 106.

71 Wendell Berry, *Sex, Economy, Freedom and Community* (New York: Pantheon, 1993), p. 139.

77 E. O. Wilson, *On Human Nature* (Cambridge, Massachusetts: Harvard University Press, 1978), p. 136.

FIDELITY

79–80 Shakespeare's sonnet is #116, available in all standard editions of his work.

88 Thomas Merton is quoted in John Howard Griffin, *A Hidden Wholeness: The Visual World of Thomas Merton* (Boston: Houghton Mifflin, 1979), p. 49.

88–89 Snyder, *A Place in Space*, pp. 43–44.

93 I quote this version of Psalm 1 from *The Book of Common Prayer* (New York: Oxford, 1990), p. 585.

94 Thomas Merton, *Faith and Violence* (Notre Dame, Indiana: Notre Dame, 1968), p. 270.

95 Havel, *Disturbing the Peace*, p. 181.

95 Mohandas K. Gandhi, *An Autobiography: The Story of My Experiments with Truth* (Boston: Beacon Press, 1957), pp. 318–19.

SKILL

105 I've written about quarriers and mill workers in my book *In Limestone Country* (Boston: Beacon Press, 1991).

105 The figure about the antiquity of stone tools comes from Jared Diamond, *The Third Chimpanzee*, p. 36.

SIMPLICITY

130   Lionel Tiger, *Optimism: The Biology of Hope* (New York: Simon & Schuster, 1979), p. 209.

132   Thoreau's call for simplicity appears in the second chapter of *Walden*, "Where I Lived and What I Lived For." See Shanley, ed., *Walden*, p. 91.

134   I quote Woolman from *The Journal of John Woolman*, ed. John Greenleaf Whittier (Secaucus, New Jersey: Citadel Press, 1972; first published 1871), pp. 200–1, 18.

135   *The Journal of John Woolman*, p. 211.

BEAUTY

147   Eudora Welty, *The Eye of the Story* (New York: Vintage, 1979), p. 105.

147   I read about the bone flute in John Noble Wilford, "Playing of Flute May Have Graced Neanderthal Fire," *New York Times*, 29 October 1996, pp. B5, B9.

151   Stephen Hawking, *A Brief History of Time* (New York: Bantam, 1988), p. 175.

151   The interview with Dennis Sciama appears in Alan Lightman and Roberta Brawer, *Origins: The Lives and Worlds of Modern Cosmologists* (Cambridge, Massachusetts: Harvard University Press, 1990), p. 153.

152   Thomas Merton, *No Man Is an Island* (New York: Harcourt Brace Jovanovich, 1955), p. 115.

152   Robinson Jeffers, *Selected Poems* (New York: Vintage, 1965), p. 94.

THE WAY OF THINGS

154   Nhat Hanh, *Living Buddha, Living Christ*, p. 21.

158–59   I quote Psalm 23:4, Isaiah 40:31, and John 3:16, from the King James Version.

162   Emerson's bold call appears in his essay "Nature" (1836), which I quote from *Emerson: Essays and Lec-*

tures, ed. Joel Porte (New York: The Library of America, 1983), p. 7.

162   Steven Weinberg, *The First Three Minutes: A Modern View of the Origin of the Universe* (New York: Basic Books, 1977), p. 154.

163   Wendell Berry, *Sex, Economy, Freedom and Community* (New York: Pantheon, 1993), p. 109.

166   Martin Buber, *I and Thou*, trans. Walter Kaufmann (New York: Scribner's, 1970), p. 174.

167   Blaise Pascal, *Selections from the Thoughts*, trans. Arthur H. Beattie (Arlington Heights, Illinois: AHM Publishing, 1965), p. 45.

168   Thoreau's advice appears in his journal for September 7, 1851. See *The Journal of Henry David Thoreau, Vol. II: 1850–September 15, 1851,* ed. Bradford Torrey and Francis H. Allen (Salt Lake City, Utah: Gibbs M. Smith, 1984; first published 1906), pp. 471–72.

Words of Thanks

I draw much of my hope from the many people who have be-friended me, put up with me, inspired and instructed me. I can list here only a few of them, and they will have to stand for the whole.

I begin as always with Ruth, my first reader, and with Eva and Jesse, my prime reasons for caring about the future, and with my mother, that earlier Eva, and my father, Greeley Sanders, who died before we could convince him why he should keep living.

I have been steadily encouraged by my colleagues in the Orion Society and by those associated with *Orion* magazine, including Chip Blake, Marion Gilliam, Laurie Lane-Zucker, Christina Rahr, Jennifer Sahn, Robert Heinzman, and George Russell. I have relished the company of my fellow troopers on Orion's Forgotten Language Tours, including Gary Nabhan, Richard Nelson, Alison Deming, Pattiann Rogers, Robert Michael Pyle, Stephanie Mills, Ann Zwinger, Kim Stafford, and Barry Lopez.

I have learned much from my students, especially those in the Wells Scholars Program at Indiana University. Also at my home university, I am grateful to Richard Stryker, Director of Overseas Study, for sending me to teach in London; to Kenneth Johnston, Chair of English, for supporting my work; to Donald Gray, John Woodcock, Tony Ardizzone, and Roger Mitchell, for bracing con-versations.

I am also grateful to those people at other institutions who gave me the chance of trying out portions of this book as talks: Scott Slovic from the Association for the Study of Literature and the Environment; Carolyn Servid and Dorik Mechau from the Island Institute; Fred Lassen from Oberlin College; Joseph

Trimmer at Ball State University; Elizabeth Dodd and Christopher Cokinos at Kansas State University; Poet Laureate Robert Hass at the Library of Congress; Joyce Dyer and David Anderson at Hiram College; John Elder at Middlebury College; Beth Daugherty and James Bailey at Otterbein College; Theresa Kemp at the University of Alabama-Birmingham; Patricia Foster at the University of Iowa; Mary Nicolini from the Indiana Teachers of Writing; Dan Shilling from the Arizona Humanities Council; Jerod Santek at The Loft in Minneapolis; Michael Collier at the Bread Loaf Writers' Conference; and George Gann from the Society for Ecological Restoration.

I warmly thank the editors of the following publications, in which earlier versions of chapters from this book first appeared: "Mountain Music I" as "Mountain Music" in Jodi Daynard, ed., *The Place Within: Portraits of the American Landscape by Twenty Contemporary Writers* (New York: Norton, 1996) and in *Orion*; "Leaping Up in Expectation" as "Hope in the Here and Now" and "Fidelity" in *Notre Dame Magazine*; "Wildness" and "Beauty" in *Orion*; "Body Bright" in *The Ohio Review*; "Skill" in *The Georgia Review*; "Simplicity" in *Audubon*; and "Mountain Music IV" as "Mountain Faith" in *Northern Lights*.

During the writing of this book, I received invaluable support from the Lannan Foundation. I am especially thankful to Jeanie Kim, Director of Literary Programs at the Foundation, for her vision and friendship. I am grateful to my agent, John Wright, for his guidance. And I give thanks once again for the keen eye and large heart of my editor at Beacon Press, Deanne Urmy.